The Balance of Nature

SIGNATURES

Senior Authors
Roger C. Farr
Dorothy S. Strickland

Authors
Richard F. Abrahamson ♦ Alma Flor Ada ♦ Barbara Bowen Coulter
Bernice E. Cullinan ♦ Margaret A. Gallego
W. Dorsey Hammond
Nancy Roser ♦ Junko Yokota ♦ Hallie Kay Yopp

Senior Consultant
Asa G. Hilliard III

Consultants
V. Kanani Choy ♦ Lee Bennett Hopkins ♦ Stephen Krashen ♦ Rosalia Salinas

Harcourt Brace & Company
Orlando Atlanta Austin Boston San Francisco Chicago Dallas New York Toronto London

Copyright © 1997 by Harcourt Brace & Company. All rights reserved. ISBN 0-15-308322-0
2 3 4 5 6 7 8 9 10   048   99 98 97

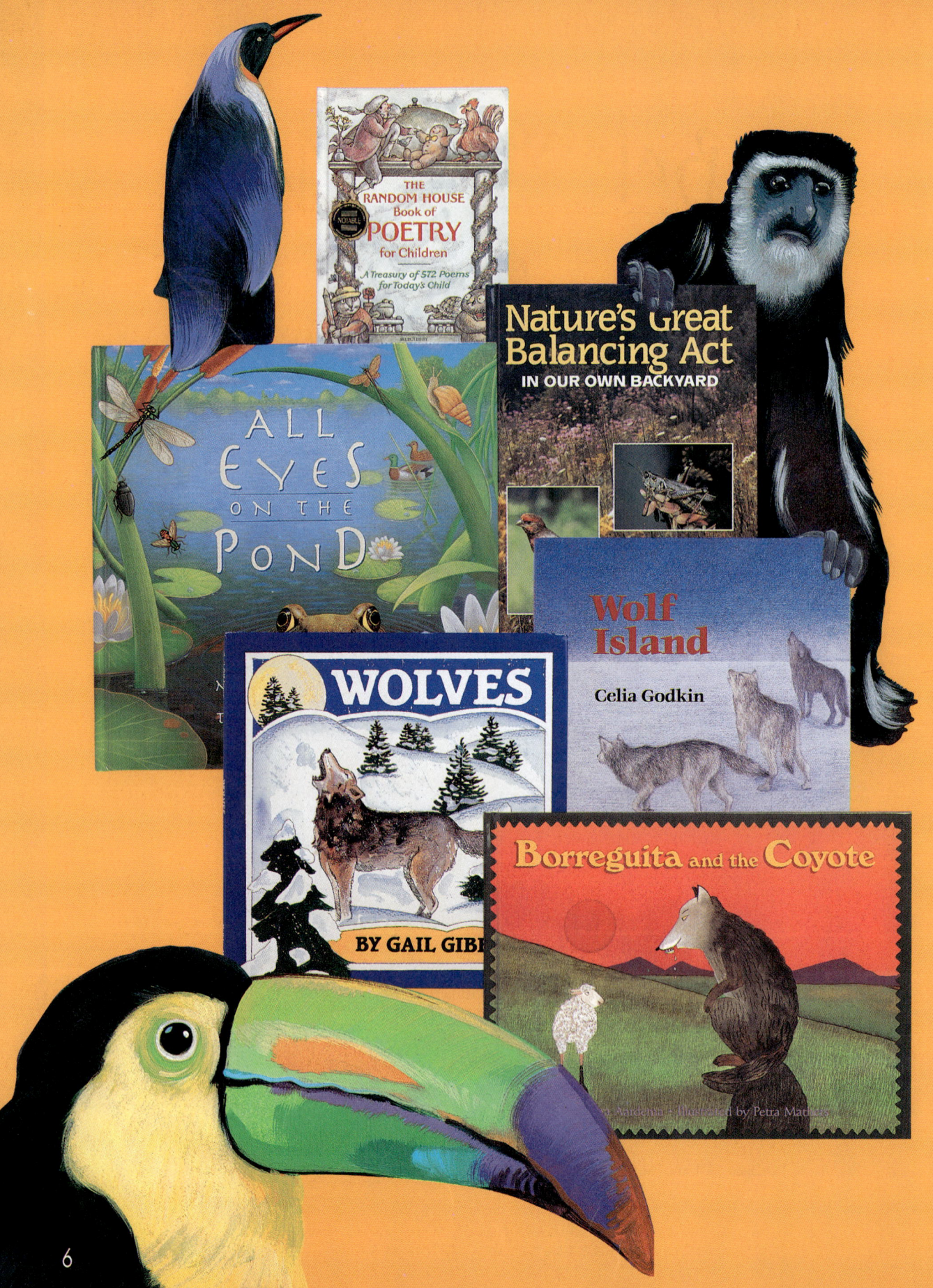

THE BALANCE OF NATURE

CONTENTS

13 Theme Opener

16 Bookshelf

Mexican Folktale/Social Studies
18 **Borreguita and the Coyote**
by Verna Aardema
illustrated by Petra Mathers
  Profile: Verna Aardema

Expository Nonfiction/Science
38 **Wolves**
written and illustrated by Gail Gibbons
  Profile: Gail Gibbons

Art
52 **Art and Literature:**
Early Autumn
by Qian Xuan

Informational Fiction/Science
54 **Wolf Island**
written and illustrated by Celia Godkin

Expository Nonfiction/Science
64 **Nature's Great Balancing Act**
by E. Jaediker Norsgaard

Poem
80 **A Bug Sat in a Silver Flower**
by Karla Kuskin

Nonfiction Verse/Science
84 **All Eyes on the Pond**
by Michael J. Rosen
illustrated by Tom Leonard
  Profile: Tom Leonard and Michael J. Rosen

108 Theme Wrap-Up

333 Glossary

7

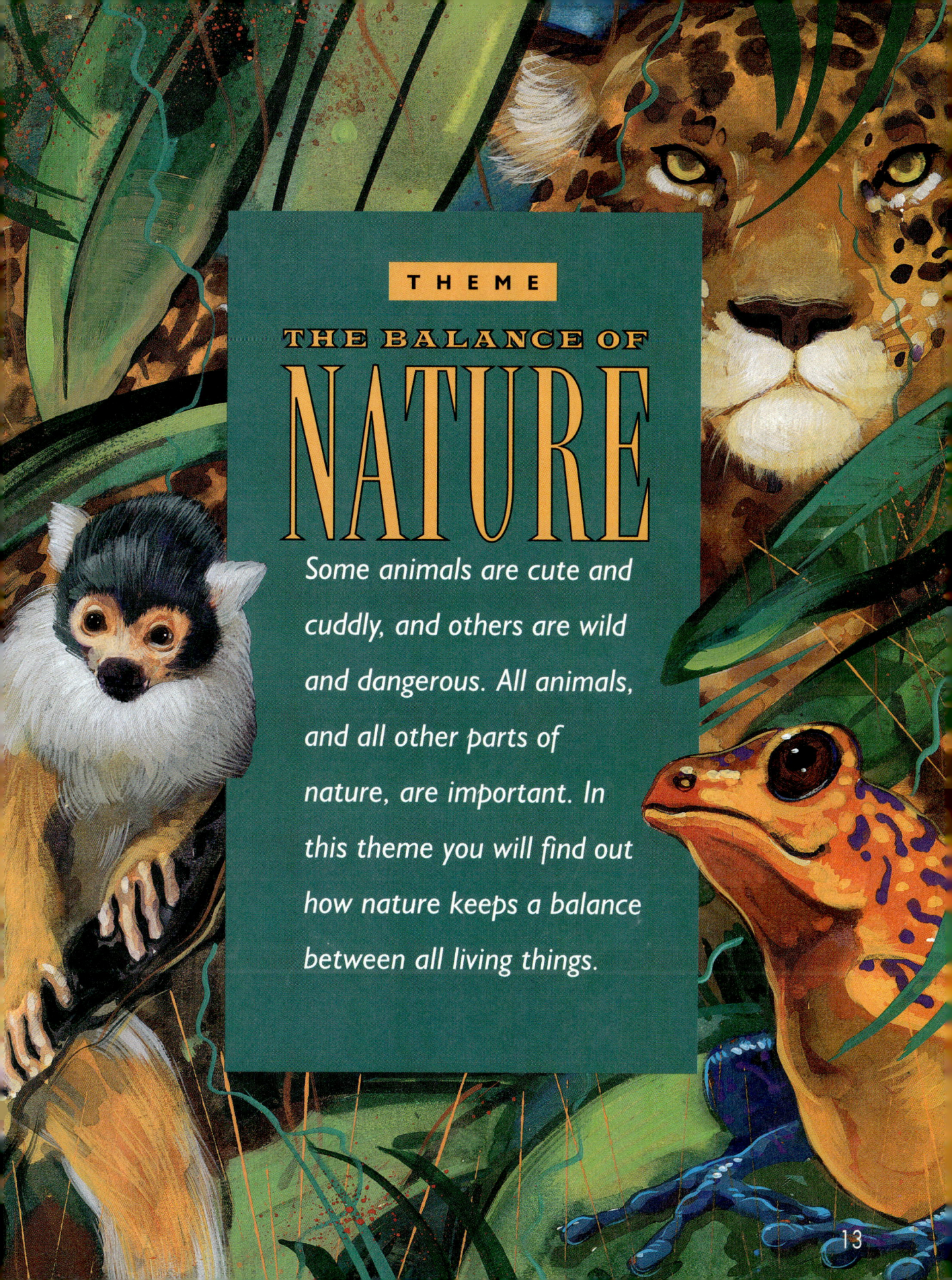

THEME

THE BALANCE OF NATURE

Some animals are cute and cuddly, and others are wild and dangerous. All animals, and all other parts of nature, are important. In this theme you will find out how nature keeps a balance between all living things.

THEME

THE BALANCE OF NATURE

CONTENTS

Borreguita and the Coyote
by Verna Aardema

Wolves
written and illustrated by Gail Gibbons

**Art and Literature:
Early Autumn**
by Qian Xuan

Wolf Island
written and illustrated by Celia Godkin

Nature's Great Balancing Act
by E. Jaediker Norsgaard

A Bug Sat in a Silver Flower
by Karla Kuskin

All Eyes on the Pond
by Michael J. Rosen

BOOKSHELF

All About Alligators
written and illustrated by Jim Arnosky

Learn what alligators look like, where they live, how they move, what they eat, and how dangerous they are.

SLJ Best Books;
Outstanding Science Trade Book

Signatures Library

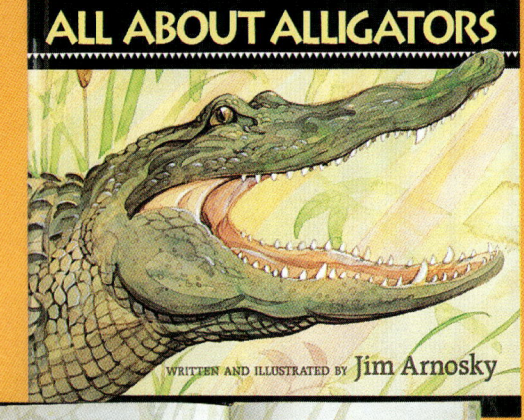

Dolphin Adventure: A True Story
by Wayne Grover

A dolphin family turns to a human diver for help in this exciting true story.

Outstanding Science Trade Book

Signatures Library

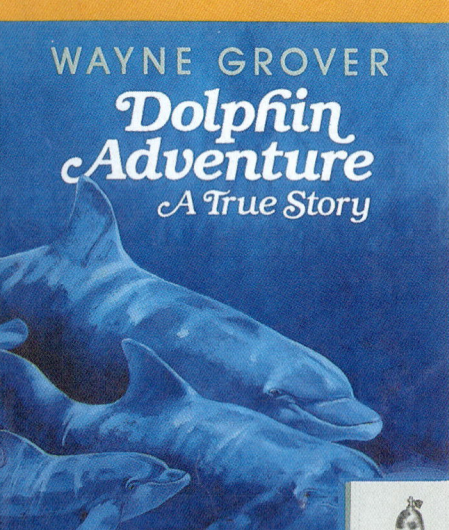
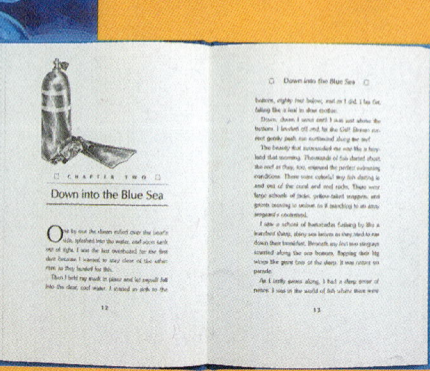
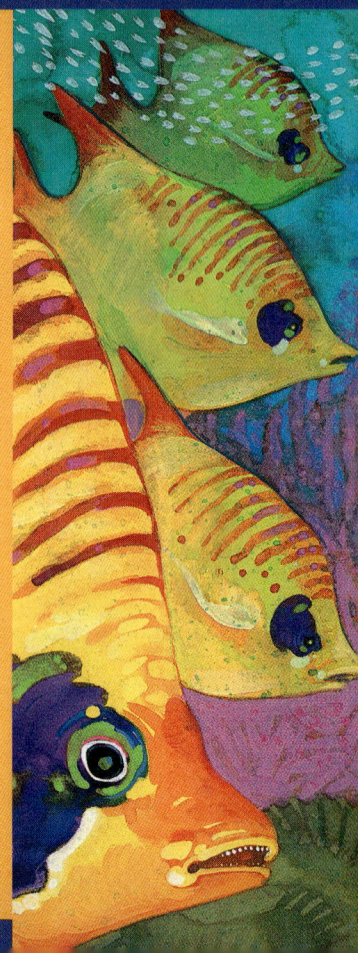

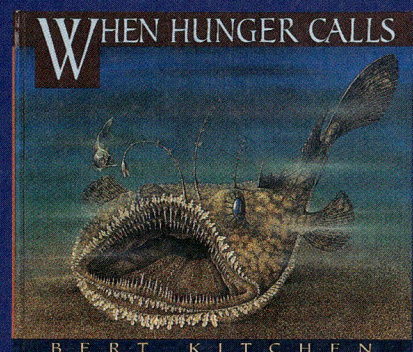

When Hunger Calls
by Bert Kitchen

Each different kind of animal has its own special skills for catching its dinner.

A Journey of Hope/Una Jornada de Esperanza
by Bob Harvey and Diane Kelsay Harvey

A baby sea turtle makes her way from the nest to the sea, in a journey filled with danger.

Outstanding Science Trade Book

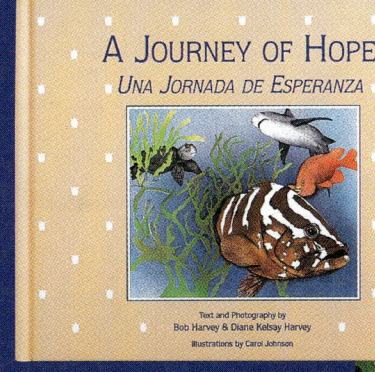

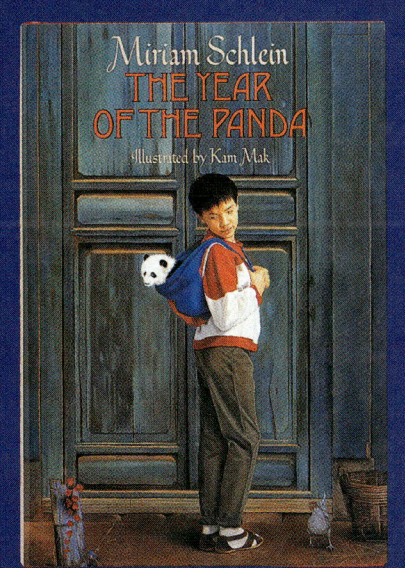

The Year of the Panda
by Miriam Schlein

Lu Yi helps to rescue a panda, and in the process he discovers a possible career for the future.

Outstanding Science Trade Book

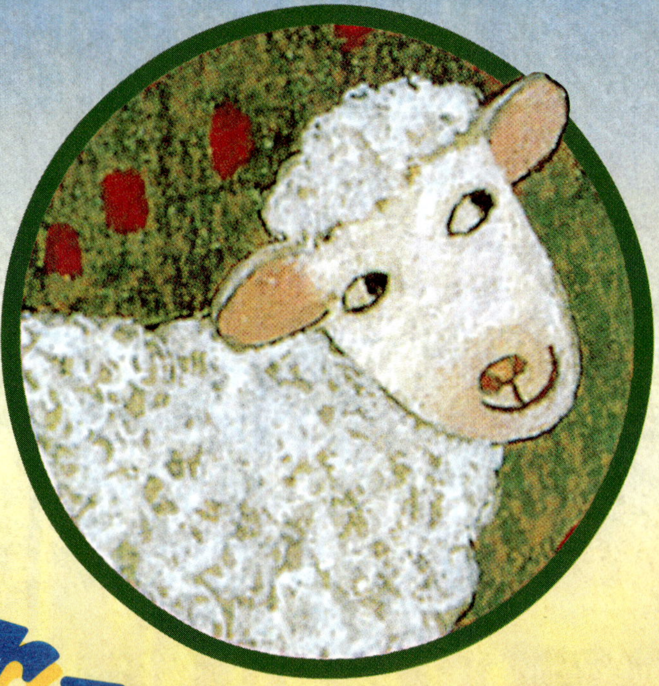

Borreguita

Borreguita and the Coyote
SLJ Best Books
Notable Trade Book
in Social Studies

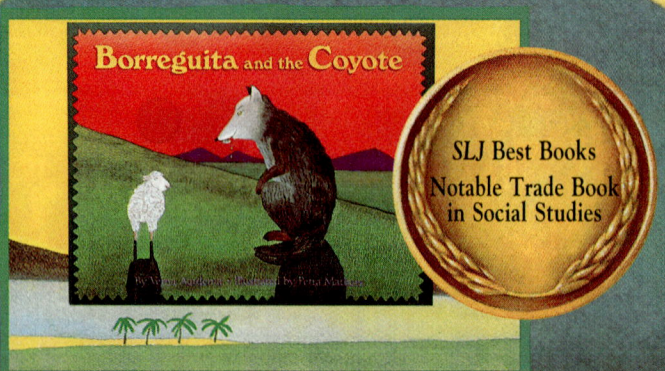

Borreguita and the Coyote
A Tale from Ayutla, Mexico

retold by Verna Aardema
illustrated by Petra Mathers

On a farm at the foot of a mountain, there once lived a little ewe lamb. Her master called her simply *Borreguita*, which means "little lamb."

One day Borreguita's master tied her to a stake in a field of red clover. The lamb was eating the lush plants when a coyote came along.

The coyote growled, "*Grrr!* Borreguita, I'm going to eat you!"

Borreguita bleated, "*Baa-a-a-a, baa-a-a-a*! Oh, Señor Coyote, I would not fill you up. I am as thin as a bean pod. When I have eaten all this clover, I shall be fat. You may eat me *then*."

Coyote looked at the skinny little lamb and the wide clover field. "*Está bien.* That is good," he said. "When you are fat, I shall come back."

After many days the coyote returned. He found the lamb grazing in a meadow. He growled, "*Grrr!* Borreguita, you are as plump as a tumbleweed. I'm going to eat you *now!*"

Borreguita bleated, *"Baa-a-a-a, baa-a-a-a!* Señor Coyote, I know something that tastes ever so much better than lamb!"

"What?" asked Coyote.

"Cheese!" cried Borreguita. "My master keeps a round of cheese on his table. He eats it on his tacos."

The coyote had never heard of cheese, and he was curious about it. "How can I get some of this cheese?" he asked.

Borreguita said, "There is a pond at the end of the pasture. Tonight, when the moon is high, meet me there. And I will show you how to get a cheese."

"Está bien," said Coyote. "I will be there."

That night, when the full moon was straight up in the sky, Borreguita and Coyote met at the edge of the pond.

There, glowing in the black water, was something that looked like a big, round cheese.

"Do you see it?" cried Borreguita. "Swim out and get it."

Coyote slipped into the water and paddled toward the cheese. He swam and swam, *shuh, shuh, shuh, shuh*. But the cheese stayed just so far ahead. Finally, he opened his mouth and lunged—WHOOOSH!

The image shattered in the splash!

Pond water rushed into Coyote's mouth. Coughing and spluttering, he turned and headed for the shore.

When he reached it, the little lamb was gone. She had tricked him! Coyote shook the water off his fur, *freh, freh, freh*.

Then he looked up at the big cheese in the sky and howled, "OWOOOOOAH!"

At dawn the next day Borreguita went to graze near a small overhanging ledge of rock on the side of the mountain. She knew that the coyote would be coming after her, and she had a plan.

 As the sun rose over the mountain, Borreguita saw the coyote coming. He was sniffing along, with his nose on some trail. She crawled under the ledge and lay on her back, bracing her feet against the top.
 When the coyote found her, he growled, "*Grrr!* Borreguita, I see you under there. I'm going to pull you out and eat you!"
 Borreguita bleated, "*Baa-a-a-a, baa-a-a-a!* Señor Coyote, you can't eat me *now*! I have to hold up this mountain. If I let go, it will come tumbling down."
 The coyote looked at the mountain. He saw that the lamb was holding it up.

"You are strong," said Borreguita. "Will you hold it while I go for help?"

The coyote did not want the mountain to fall, so he crept under the ledge and put up his feet.

"Push hard," said Borreguita. "Do you have it now?"

"I have it," said Coyote. "But hurry back. This mountain is heavy."

Borreguita rolled out of the shallow cave and went leaping and running all the way back to the barnyard.

Coyote held up that rock until his legs ached and he was hungry and thirsty. At last he said, "Even if the mountain falls, I'm going to let go! I can't hold it any longer."

The coyote dragged himself out and covered his head with his paws. The mountain did not fall. Then he knew—the little lamb had fooled him again.

Coyote sat on his haunches and howled, "OWOOOOOAH!"

Early the next morning the coyote hid himself in a thicket in the lamb's pasture. When she drew near, he sprang out with a WOOF! And he said, "Borreguita, you will not escape this time! I'm going to eat you *now*!"

Borreguita bleated, *"Baa-a-a-a, baa-a-a-a!* Señor Coyote, I know I deserve to die. But grant me one kindness. Swallow me whole so that I won't have to suffer the biting and the chewing."

"Why should I make you comfortable while I eat you?" demanded the coyote. "Anyway, I couldn't swallow you all in one piece even if I wanted to."

"Oh, yes, you could!" cried Borreguita. "Your mouth is so big, you could swallow a cougar. Open it wide, and I will run and dive right in."

Coyote opened his mouth wide and braced his feet. Borreguita backed away. Then she put her head down and charged. BAM! She struck the inside of Coyote's mouth so hard she sent him rolling.

"OW, OW, OW!" howled the coyote as he picked himself up and ran away—his mouth feeling like one big toothache!

And from that day on, Borreguita frisked about on the farm at the foot of the mountain. And Coyote never bothered her again.

**THE END
FIN**

Meet the Author: Verna Aardema

As a child, Verna Aardema loved to read. Her family often had a hard time tearing her away from the book she was reading at the time—even when she had to help out around the house!

When Verna was in the sixth grade, she wrote a poem that she was very proud of. As soon as Verna's mother read it, she knew her daughter would be a writer. From then on, Verna's mother encouraged her daughter whenever she could. Verna would run out the door right after dinner and go to a nearby swamp to think about the things she wanted to write. Soon, she was making up stories and telling them to the kids in her neighborhood.

Verna Aardema has now written more than twenty books for children, retelling popular folktales. Like most authors, she spends time revising her work. See the next page, which shows an early draft of "Borreguita and the Coyote."

"Writing is not easy but the rewards are great! When starry-eyed boys and girls tell me they want to be authors, I hug them for success."

Borreguita and the Coyote
A Tale from Ayutla
Mexico

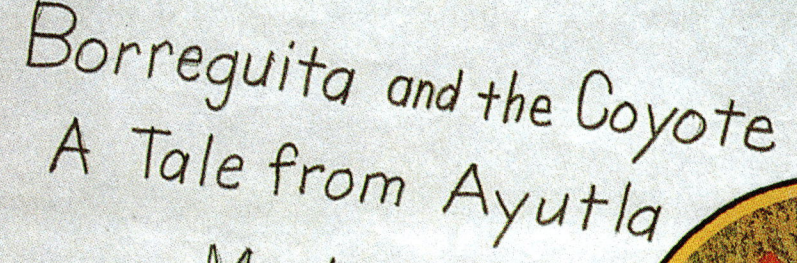

On a farm at the foot of a mountain in Mexico, there once lived a little ewe lamb. Her master called her simply *Borreguita*, which means "little lamb."

One day Borreguita's master tied her to a stake in an alfalfa field. The lamb was eating the lush green plants when a coyote came along.

The coyote said, "Borreguita, I'm going to eat you!"

Borreguita bleated, "BA-A-A, BA-A-A! Oh, Señor Coyote, I would not fill you up. I am thin as a bean pod. When I have eaten all this alfalfa, I shall be fat. You may eat me then."

Coyote looked at the skinny little lamb and the wide alfalfa field. "*Está bien*. That is good," he said. "When you are fat, I shall come back."

After many days the coyote returned. He found the lamb grazing in a meadow. He said, "Borreguita, you are as plump as a tumbleweed. I'm going to eat you now!"

"Señor Coyote," cried Borreguita, "I know something that tastes ever so much better than lamb!"

"What?" asked Coyote.

"Cheese!" cried Borreguita. "My master keeps a round of cheese on his table. He eats it on his tacos."

The coyote had never heard of cheese, and he was curious about it. "How can I get some of this cheese?" he asked.

Borreguita said, "There is a pond at the end of the pasture. Tonight, when the moon is high, meet me there. And I will show you how to get a cheese."

"*Está bien*," said Coyote. "I will be there."

That night, when the full moon was straight up in the sky, Borreguita and Coyote met at the edge of the pond.

There, glowing in the black water, was something that looked like a big, round cheese.

"Do you see it?" cried Borreguita. "Swim out and get it."

Coyote slipped into the water and paddled toward the cheese. He swam and swam, but the cheese stayed just so far ahead. Finally, he opened his mouth and lunged—WHOOSH!

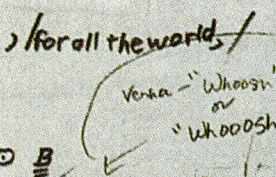

Response Corner

WRITE A POSTCARD

Postcards from Ayutla

Look in an atlas for a map of Mexico. Use the index to help you locate the city of Ayutla. Notice the landforms and bodies of water nearby. What would you see if you visited Ayutla? Write a postcard describing the area to your friends back home. On the front of your postcard, draw a scene that you might see in Ayutla.

MAKE A LIST

Brains or Brawn?

Like "Borreguita and the Coyote," many other stories have one character who is weak but successful. With a classmate, make a list of story characters like Borreguita, who were more successful than a stronger character. For each character, write a sentence telling what qualities helped him or her to succeed.

WRITE A SHORT STORY

The Moral of the Story...

Coyote finally learned his lesson after many troubles. Think about a lesson you learned the hard way. Then write a one-page short story with a moral, or lesson, at the end. Draw pictures to go with your story. You and your classmates may want to make a book of your stories.

What Do You Think?

▼ How does Borreguita outsmart Coyote?

▼ What is your favorite illustration in this story? Describe what it shows, and tell why you like it.

▼ Coyote is a character in many Native American and Mexican stories. What is he like in this story?

Wolves

BY GAIL GIBBONS

Award-Winning Author and Illustrator

GRAY WOLF OR TIMBER WOLF

It is a snowy moonlit night in the northern woods. An animal shakes the snow from its thick fur, throws its head back and joins its companions in a long howl. The animal is a wolf.

There are two different types of wolves. One is the gray wolf, or timber wolf. A gray wolf can have black, white, brown or gray fur depending on where it lives. Thirty-two different kinds of gray wolves have been identified. Some of them don't exist anymore.

RED WOLF

The other type of wolf is the red wolf. Red wolves aren't really red. Instead, they are the combination of black, gray and reddish brown. They are smaller and more slender than gray wolves. Only one of the three original different kinds of red wolves exists today. Very few of them live in the wild.

The first ancestors of wolves lived more than 50 million years ago. Over time, these creatures developed into wolves.

Wolves are members of the dog family, called Canidae. All dogs are related to wolves.

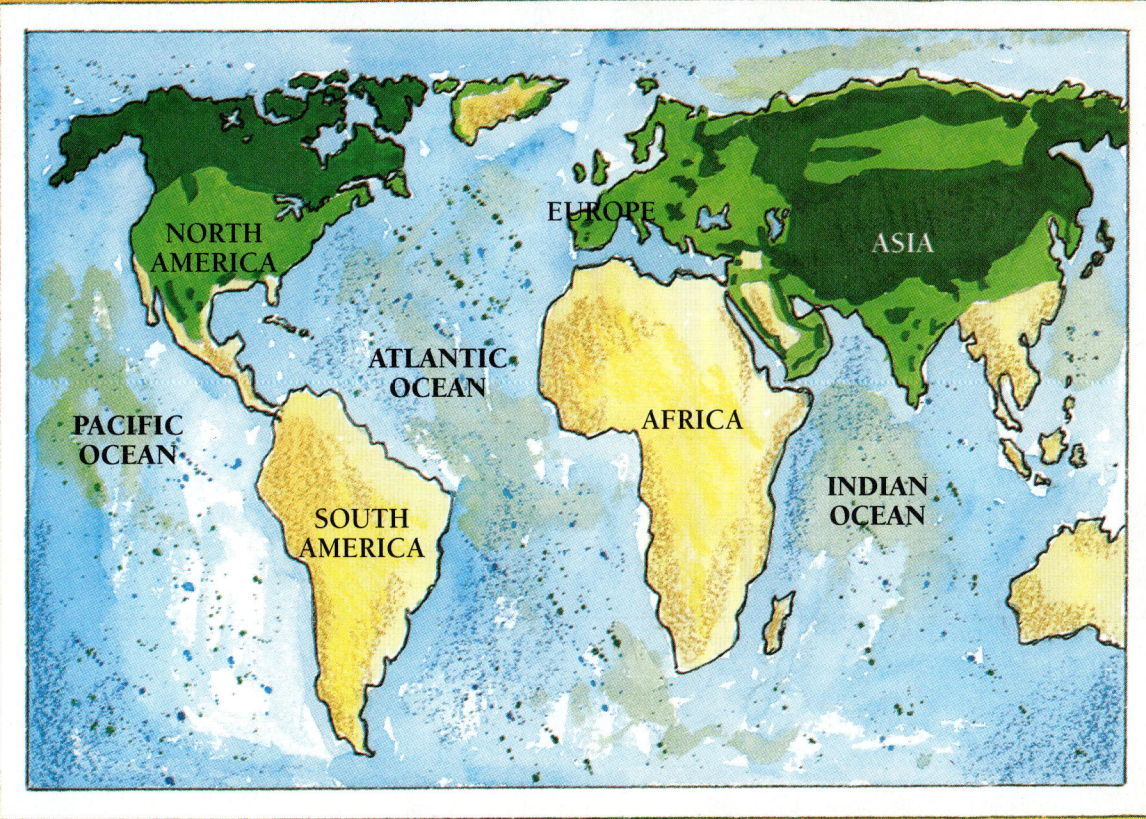

☐ WHERE WOLVES ONCE LIVED   ■ WHERE WOLVES LIVE TODAY

A few hundred years ago, wolves lived all around the world. People hunted them and also took over much of their territory. There were fewer wolves and they moved away. Today most wolves are found in the northern parts of the world.

Most male wolves weigh more than 100 pounds. The females weigh less. Wolves are very strong and have long legs, a long tail, and are covered with fur.

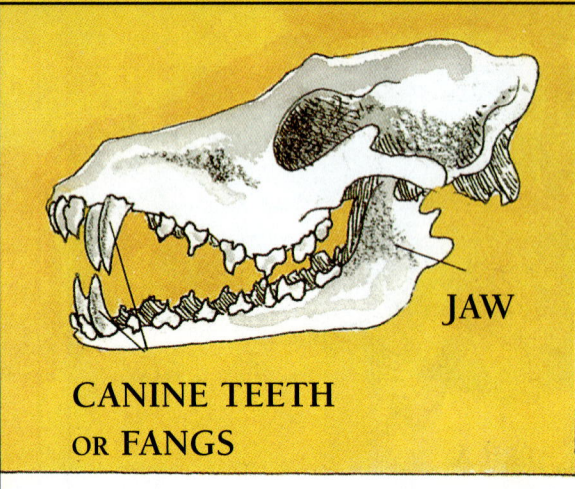

CANINE TEETH OR FANGS — **JAW**

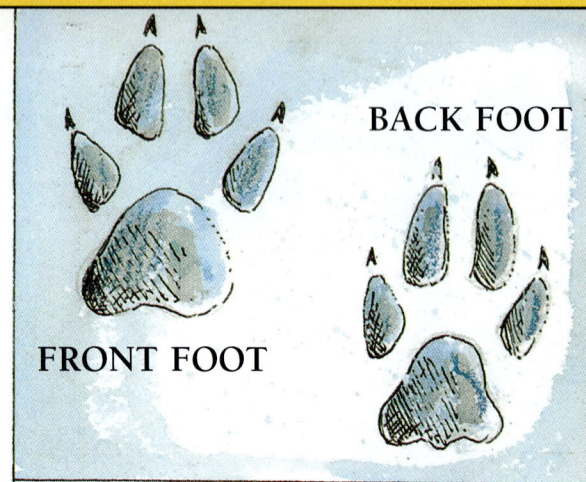

FRONT FOOT — **BACK FOOT**

Wolves are hunters. They are carnivores, which means they eat meat. They have strong jaws and forty-two teeth for tearing, chewing and grinding. Four of the teeth are called canine teeth, or fangs. Wolves use their canine teeth to grip an animal when they catch it.

Wolves have a keen sense of smell for sniffing out their prey. They can hear sounds from far away, too. When wolves roam, they leave big paw prints behind. Some tracks can be as large as a grownup's hand.

Gray wolves live in groups called packs. These packs can be made up of three to more than twenty wolves. It is believed that red wolves don't form packs. Wolf packs live and hunt in territories which can cover an area as big as 500 square miles. They mark the boundaries with their urine, which leaves a scent that warns other wolf packs to stay away. Each pack has adult males and females, and their pups.

The leader of a pack is called an alpha wolf. An alpha wolf is smart and strong. He will fight any wolf that tries to take over his pack. The alpha wolf is the tallest in the pack. When he looks the other wolves in the eye, they crouch down and tuck their tails between their hind legs. Sometimes they roll over and lick the alpha wolf's face, letting him know he's boss.

The members of a pack care for each other. They protect each other when other wolf packs try to invade their territory. They hunt and share their food together, too. The alpha wolf decides where and when to hunt. It would be difficult for a wolf to catch a big animal alone. Hunting in packs helps them survive.

Once they spot their prey, the chase begins. Wolves' legs are built for speed and running long distances. Often, an animal outruns them. Other times the prey tires and slows down.

The pack fans out in a circle around the animal. Then one wolf charges and attacks the animal. It hangs on tightly. Others attack.

Soon the fight is over. The hungry wolves can eat. Wolves hunt many different kinds of animals like moose, deer and caribou. They also hunt smaller animals such as rabbits, beavers and small rodents.

WHIMPER

SNARL

WOOF

BARK

Wolves make different sounds to "talk" to each other. They whimper when they are excited or restless. A snarl means the wolf is being threatened. A short woof is a warning, and a bark means danger is near.

Wolves howl, too. The sound is eerie and sometimes seems sad. They howl to tell other packs to stay out of their territory. Often, it is the way they stay in touch with the others in their pack when they are separated. Sometimes they howl before a hunt.

Wolves communicate in other ways, too. They show their teeth when they are angry. When a wolf is scared, its ears go flat against its head. A wagging tail means the wolf is happy. If just the tip of the tail wags, it could be ready to attack.

Wolves often mate for life. Wolf pups are born in the spring. The alpha female is the only one of the females in a pack to give birth to a litter of pups. There can be three to fourteen pups. They only weigh about one pound at birth and cannot see or hear. They nuzzle up against their mother to drink her milk in the den where they live.

When the pups are about three weeks old, they are allowed out of their den to romp and play. The mother and some of the other wolves take turns babysitting while the rest of the pack is hunting. When the hunters return, the pups greet them. When they lick the wolves' jaws, the wolves bring up some of the food they have eaten and feed it to the pups. The pups are now old enough to eat meat.

At six months old the pups are almost as big as the adult wolves. They are strong enough and old enough to begin learning how to hunt. They join the pack as it roams in search of food.

For centuries people have been afraid of wolves. They thought wolves were their enemies. Scientists who study wolves are learning that wolves have been misunderstood. Wolves tend to live peacefully among themselves. They are shy and rarely attack people. When this happens, they have probably been threatened.

When wolves hunt, often the animals they kill are weak and sickly. The healthy and stronger animals survive. Wolves are not cruel. They are just very efficient hunters.

Occasionally wolves attack farm or ranch animals. This can make the farmers or ranchers want to kill them. Wolves are hunted for their fur, too.

Because wolves are in danger of extinction, some people realize they must be protected. Some scientists and people who work at zoos help wolves by raising them so they can be released into the wild. In many parts of the world laws have been passed making it illegal to hunt wolves.

By studying wolves in their natural surroundings and watching them for long periods of time, scientists have learned that wolves play an important part in the balance of our natural world. The old fears and myths about wolves are dying. Wolves deserve to live undisturbed.

If enough people care, there will be wild wolves for years to come, and the howling sounds these beautiful creatures make will still be heard.

MORE WAYS OF THE WOLVES

Wolves are the largest of the wild dogs, which include coyotes, foxes, and others.

Wolves have very few enemies. These enemies can be other packs of wolves, bears, and people.

Wolves usually trot or run in a way called loping. They are very fast runners. Some can run up to forty miles per hour.

A pack of howling wolves can be heard from as far away as ten miles.

When wolves hunt in snow, they walk in single file. They take turns making tracks for the others to walk in.

Wolves vary in size. The smallest kind in the world is the Arabian wolf. It is only about 32 inches long.

In North America there is no record of a healthy wolf ever attacking a person.

Some experts believe ancient people learned how to hunt by watching packs of wolves hunt.

Wolves are good swimmers but rarely follow prey into water during a chase.

In captivity, wolves have been known to live up to seventeen years. In the wild, life is much harder. Wolves usually live to be only nine to ten years old.

GAIL GIBBONS
Talks About Wolves

Our family lives out in the country in Vermont. When my daughter was about twelve, she saw a wolf as she was coming home from school. It startled her, and then it ran away. Actually, they both ran. My daughter ran into the house while the wolf ran into the woods.

Around the same time, I noticed several articles in the newspaper about wolves. One was about wolves in Alaska, and the other was about putting wolves back into the national forests. There are so many myths about wolves that I decided to write a book about them and find out the truth for myself.

When I write, I do the research for the book first. Also, it's very important for me to actually see what I'm writing about. For this book, I spent time at the Bronx Zoo, where I observed wolves.

After I've done my research and written the book, I find an expert who can help me check my work. For me, a book takes about a year from the time I get an idea to the time I send it off to my editor. Usually, I'm working on several books at once.

Response

WRITE A STORY

THE REAL STORY

You read in the selection that there are many myths about wolves that are not true. Write a short story that helps show the truth about wolves. You might make the main character a wolf who is in danger. Help your reader see some good things about wolves.

WRITE AN AD

A WOLF'S FRIEND

Lawmakers and scientists are just some of the people who are trying to protect wolves. Study advertisements in a newspaper. Then write your own ad, asking for volunteers to help save wolves. Try to make people see that this project is important.

Corner

MAKE A POSTER

SAFETY IN THE WILD

Many people want to save wolves. Others, such as hikers and campers, may fear them. People in forest areas need to be very careful because wild animals can be dangerous. Make a poster of safety tips to help people be safe around wild animals.

WHAT DO YOU THINK?

- How does Gail Gibbons feel about wolves? How do you know?

- What else would you like to know about wolves? Where could you find that information?

- Should animals always be allowed to roam wherever they want? Why or why not?

51

ART & LITERATURE

In this theme, you have been reading about how animals survive in nature. How is this Chinese painting like the selections you have read? Why do you think the frog is watching the dragonflies?

The Detroit Institute of Arts; Founders Society Purchase.

EARLY AUTUMN

by Qian Xuan

Qian Xuan painted this picture about seven hundred years ago. Artists at that time used brushes dipped in different ink colors to make their paintings. They spoke of "writing" a painting.

Wolf Island

by Celia Godkin

Outstanding Science Trade Book

Once there was an island. It was an island with trees and meadows, and many kinds of animals. There were mice, rabbits and deer, squirrels, foxes and several kinds of birds.

All the animals on the island depended on the plants and the other animals for their food and well-being. Some animals ate grass or other plants; some ate insects; some ate other animals. The island animals were healthy. There was plenty of food for all.

A family of wolves lived on the island, too, a male wolf, a female, and their five cubs.

One day the wolf cubs were playing on the beach while their mother and father slept. The cubs found a strange object at the edge of the water.

Wolf Island

Celia Godkin

It was a log raft, nailed together with boards. The cubs had never seen anything like this before. They were very curious. They climbed onto it and sniffed about. Everything smelled different.

While the cubs were poking around, the raft began to drift slowly out into the lake. At first the cubs didn't notice anything wrong. Then, suddenly, there was nothing but water all around the raft.

The cubs were scared. They howled. The mother and father wolf heard the howling and came running down to the water's edge.

They couldn't turn the raft back, and the cubs were too scared to swim, so the adult wolves swam out to the raft and climbed aboard. The raft drifted slowly and steadily over to the mainland. Finally it came to rest on the shore and the wolf family scrambled onto dry land.

There were no longer wolves on the island.

Time passed. Spring grew into summer on the island, and summer into fall. The leaves turned red. Geese flew south, and squirrels stored up nuts for the winter.

Winter was mild that year, with little snow. The green plants were buried under a thin white layer. Deer dug through the snow to find food. They had enough to eat.

Next spring, many fawns were born.

There were now many deer on the island. They were eating large amounts of grass and leaves. The wolf family had kept the deer population down, because wolves eat deer for food. Without wolves to hunt the deer, there were now too many deer on the island for the amount of food available.

Spring grew into summer and summer into fall. More and more deer ate more and more grass and more and more leaves.

Rabbits had less to eat, because the deer were eating their food. There were not many baby bunnies born that year.

Foxes had less to eat, because there were fewer rabbits for them to hunt.

Mice had less to eat, because the deer had eaten the grass and grass seed. There were not many baby mice born that year.

Owls had less to eat, because there were fewer mice for them to hunt. Many animals on the island were hungry.

The first snow fell. Squirrels curled up in their holes, wrapped their tails around them for warmth, and went to sleep. The squirrels were lucky. They had collected a store of nuts for winter.

Other animals did not have winter stores. They had to find food in the snow. Winter is a hard time for animals, but this winter was harder than most. The snow was deep and the weather cold. Most of the plants had already been eaten during the summer and fall. Those few that remained were hard to find, buried deep under the snow.

Rabbits were hungry. Foxes were hungry. Mice were hungry. Owls were hungry. Even the deer were hungry. The whole island was hungry.

The owls flew over to the mainland, looking for mice. They flew over the wolf family walking along the mainland shore. The wolves were thin and hungry, too. They had not found a home, because there were other wolf families on the mainland. The other wolves did not want to share with them.

Snow fell for many weeks. The drifts became deeper and deeper. It was harder and harder for animals to find food. Animals grew weaker, and some began to die. The deer were so hungry they gnawed bark from the trees. Trees began to die.

Snow covered the island. The weather grew colder and colder. Ice began to form in the water around the island, and along the mainland coast. It grew thicker and thicker, spreading farther and farther out into the open water. One day there was ice all the way from the mainland to the island.

The wolf family crossed the ice and returned to their old home.

The wolves were hungry when they reached the island, and there were many weak and sick deer for them to eat. The wolves left the healthy deer alone.

Finally, spring came. The snow melted, and grass and leaves began to grow. The wolves remained in their island home, hunting deer. No longer would there be too many deer on the island. Grass and trees would grow again. Rabbits would find enough food. The mice would find enough food. There would be food for the foxes and owls. And there would be food for the deer. The island would have food enough for all.

Life on the island was back in balance.

Nature's Great Balancing Act

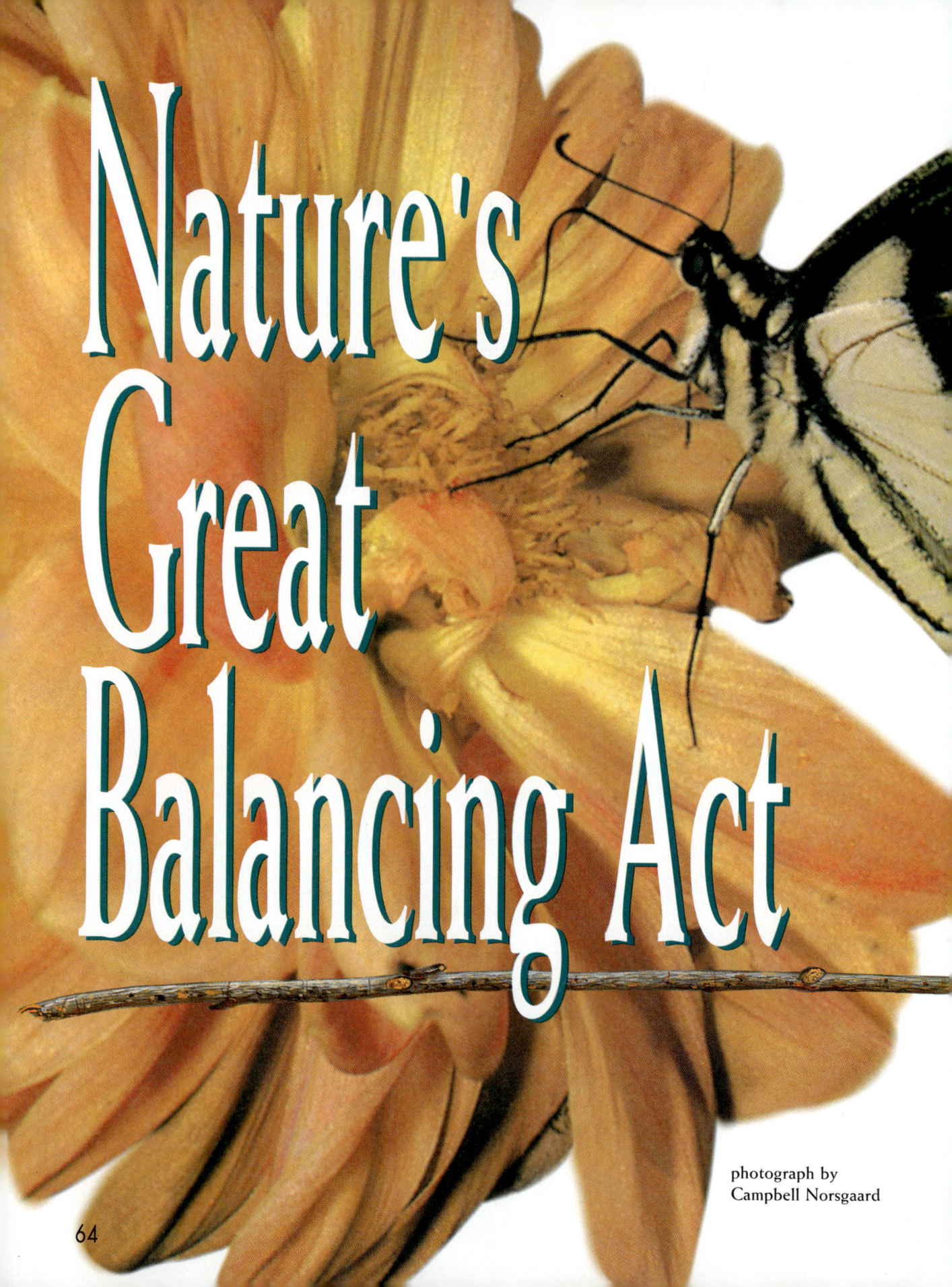

photograph by
Campbell Norsgaard

IN OUR OWN BACKYARD

BY E. JAEDIKER NORSGAARD

Outstanding Science Trade Book

Welcome to our backyard!

You won't find a tame grass carpet, but a large semi-wild wonderland that stretches from our house to the bordering woods. Some years ago we decided to let everything grow as it pleases. Now it's a community where many of our fellow creatures are at home. On a summer day, grasshoppers will jump away from your footsteps. You'll see bees buzzing around raspberry bushes, butterflies landing on wildflowers, birds feeding insects to their young. There are chipmunks and a family of bold raccoons. Deer venture out of the woods to nibble hedges and shrubs.

photograph by Campbell Norsgaard

All creatures in the animal kingdom depend on plants and on each other for survival, one feeding on another. They are all parts of a gigantic puzzle in which the pieces fit together but, like a kaleidoscope, are forever changing. You are a mammal, and you are a part of that puzzle too, though you are quite different from other mammals and from birds, reptiles, amphibians, and insects. All living things are members of nature's great balancing act. You can see how this works right here in our own backyard.

FOOD CHAINS

Nature's great balancing act depends on food chains. All food chains begin with plants. Plants are able to make their own food, using energy from the sun, and they pass that energy on to animals that eat them. Plants are the basis of all the food and energy that you and other animals use.

When an animal eats a plant or eats another animal, it becomes part of a food chain. In our backyard, as well as everywhere else, all food chains begin with plant-eaters (herbivores) and usually end with a meat-eater (carnivore). Food chains can be short or as long as five or six links. If you eat

Like many mammals, this red fox eats plants and animals.

an apple, that is a two-link food chain. If you eat meat from a sheep or cow that has eaten plants, that is a three-link food chain. You are at the top of those food chains.

Here in the backyard, one food chain might begin with a moth sipping nectar from a flower. The moth is caught by a sparrow and fed to its young in the nest in our hedge. The young bird might be taken from its nest and eaten by a raccoon. The raccoon is at the top of this food chain. There are no predators[1] in the backyard to eat the raccoon.

---

[1] **predators**: animals that live by eating other animals

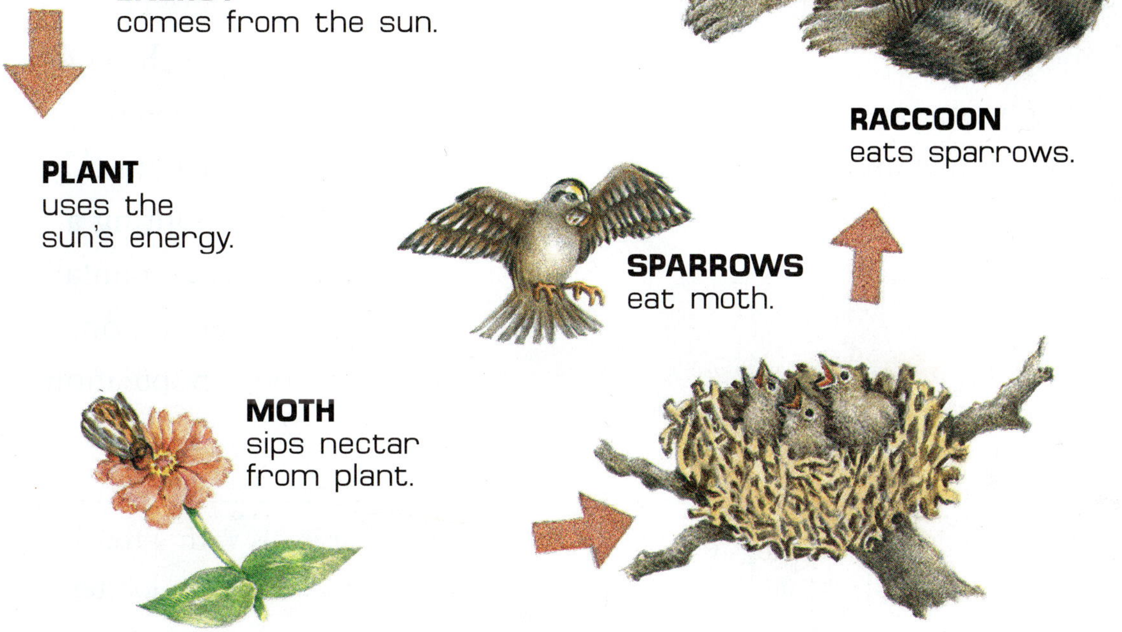

ENERGY comes from the sun.

PLANT uses the sun's energy.

MOTH sips nectar from plant.

SPARROWS eat moth.

RACCOON eats sparrows.

Another food chain might start with a fly feeding on decaying vegetation[2] in the backyard. The fly is caught and eaten by a spider. The spider is eaten by a toad, which is eaten by a fox.

First links in any food chain are usually the smallest but most abundant plants and animals. Microscopic green algae and other plant plankton[3] float in the ponds, lakes, and seas. They are eaten in great quantities by water insects and small crustaceans,[4] which are eaten by small fishes, which are, in turn, eaten by larger fishes that may end up on your dinner table.

Each time an animal eats a plant or one animal eats another, a tiny bit of the sun's energy is passed along the food chain. Each animal uses some of that energy and passes along what is left. Amazingly, the used energy is not destroyed, only changed into other forms or passed into the atmosphere.[5]

BALANCING POPULATIONS

Animal populations are kept in balance by the amount of food available and by predators in the food chain. Take mice, for instance. You can't really catch sight of them scurrying through the tall grass in the backyard, eating seeds. They move quickly to avoid enemies. During a summer of heavy rainfall and lush vegetation, the mouse population

---

[2] **decaying vegetation**: rotting plants
[3] **algae and plant plankton**: simple plants that float or drift in the water

[4] **crustaceans**: animals with a tough shell that live in water, like lobsters and crabs
[5] **atmosphere**: the air around the earth

This long-eared owl helps keep the mouse population in balance.

increases, providing more food for hawks and owls and other mouse-eaters. When less food is available, mice tend to raise fewer young. This affects the numbers of hawks and owls also. If the insect and rodent populations decrease,[6] owls and hawks raise fewer young or find better territory or else starve. A balance of numbers is maintained.

Some farmers shoot hawks and owls, believing that they kill a few chickens. But without these predators, rabbits and mice overpopulate and spread into cultivated fields to eat corn, wheat, oats, rye, barley, rice, and sugar cane—the grasses which are first links in human food chains. This is what happens when we upset a balanced community.

---

[6] **decrease**: to go down in size or number

FEATHERED HELPERS

Birds are a great help in keeping the numbers of insects in balance.

The friendly chickadees are greeting us from the lilac bushes, with their cheerful call . . . dee-dee-dee . . . between dashes to the feeder for sunflower seeds, or excursions into the brush for caterpillars and other insects and spiders.

A couple of barn swallows are catching winged insects to feed their babies in a mud-and-straw nest on a high beam in our garden tool shed.

These newly hatched barn swallows rely on their parents for food.

A pair of cardinals is swooping down on grasshoppers. I can't help hoping that no snake or owl raids their nest in the hedge, but that's a possibility.

The tiny house wren parents are tireless hunters, making continuous trips from dawn until dark to satisfy the high-pitched hunger cries of their babies in the nest box near our kitchen window. A young bird may eat its weight in insects every day!

In the spring, we watch the birds compete for inchworms, hopping from twig to twig, picking the leaves clean.

We saw the female Baltimore oriole peel dried fibers off last year's tall dogbane plant with her beak and fly high up in the oak tree to weave them into her nest. She and the male who courted and won her fed their nestlings with soft parts of insects, and themselves ate caterpillars, beetles, wasps, grasshoppers, and ants.

Young blue jays with innocent faces and fresh white and blue feathers follow their parents around, fluttering their wings to be fed, although they've grown as large as the adults.

Birds are a joy to watch as they go about their business, protecting the plants in our backyards and gardens from an oversupply of leaf-eating insects.

This young blue jay is not yet ready to hunt for its own food.

Too many grasshoppers can be harmful to a garden.

73

MAMMALS

A family of deer often comes out of the small woods bordering our backyard and browses among the plants. When we go outside, they stop and stare at us with wide eyes, then turn and leap gracefully away, wiggling their white tails.

In winter, they walk through the snow up to the house itself to nibble hedges and shrubs. Deer can double their numbers in a single year. Long ago, their populations were kept in check mainly by cougars (mountain lions) that leaped on them from low tree limbs. And by packs of wolves, and by native American Indians who hunted them for food, buckskins, and doeskins. Today, without predators except man in many places, deer sometimes eat every leaf and bud in their range, and some starve in winter.

Without predators, these deer can upset the balance of nature.

75

The lively little chipmunks have found an easy way to make a living. Besides collecting wild plant seeds, one is sitting near the bird feeder, stuffing so many fallen sunflower seeds into his mouth that the pouches in his cheeks puff up like small balloons. He races to his underground nest to store them away and is soon back for more, running quickly to avoid hawks and other predators.

Chipmunks store nuts and seeds for the cold winter months ahead.

A red fox sometimes walks stealthily into our backyard at sunset, hunting mice and birds. The chipmunks dart into their burrows where they're safe from the fox, but not from weasels.

As we wait for more furry visitors, the evening air is filled with scraping sounds of katydids calling their own names, and the high jingle bell chorus of snowy tree crickets. They feed on the foliage[7] in which they hide, daring to advertise for mates at night when the birds that prey on them are asleep.

---

[7] **foliage**: the leaves on trees and plants

Katydids hide from their enemies by blending in with leaves and branches.

A family of raccoons and an opossum make trails through the backyard, stopping to munch berries. This is part of their regular rounds as they seek out mice, lizards, grasshoppers, and crickets, and grub in the mud for frogs.

Opossums eat many different kinds of animals.

Frogs live in the mud and can catch flying insects with their long tongues.

In case they're still hungry, the raccoons are bold enough to look in our kitchen window or tap on the door and invite themselves in for a snack. The opossum, who eats almost anything, gets in on the act. After all, humans have taken over much of their territory.

This bold raccoon is looking for a snack in an unusual place!

A Bug Sat in a Silver Flower

by Karla Kuskin
illustrated by Daniel Moreton

Award-Winning Poet

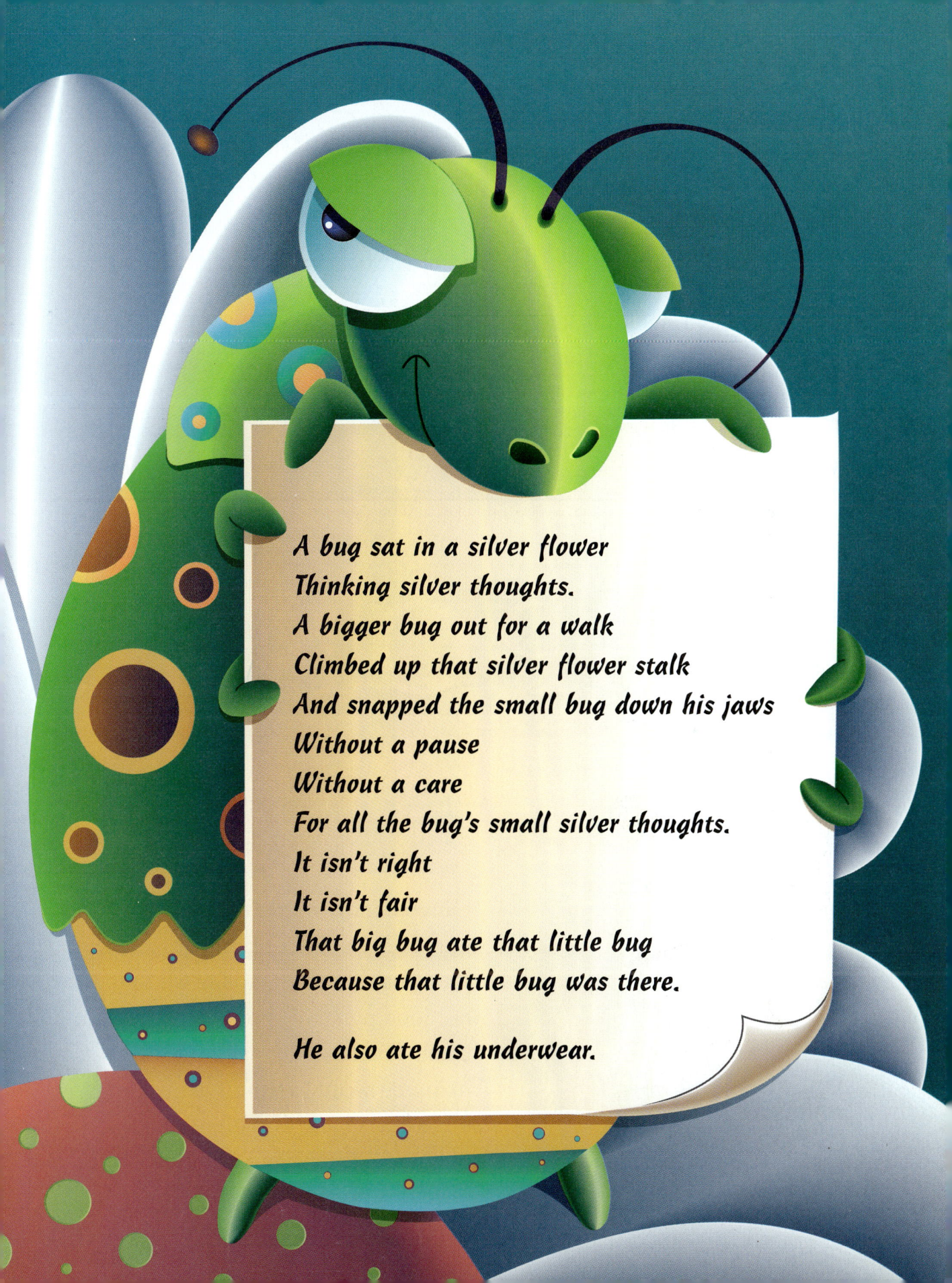

A bug sat in a silver flower
Thinking silver thoughts.
A bigger bug out for a walk
Climbed up that silver flower stalk
And snapped the small bug down his jaws
Without a pause
Without a care
For all the bug's small silver thoughts.
It isn't right
It isn't fair
That big bug ate that little bug
Because that little bug was there.

He also ate his underwear.

WRITE A NEWS STORY

THIS JUST IN...

Write a television news story for the Backyard News Network (BNN). Give the latest facts on the crime described in "A Bug Sat in a Silver Flower." Has the big bug been caught? Where was he last seen? Read your bulletin to your classmates.

RESPONSE

WRITE MENUS

PYRAMIDS ARE NOT JUST IN EGYPT

Do you know where to find a food pyramid? It's not a place you visit. It's a healthful eating plan. Study the food pyramid shown on a food label. Then use the pyramid to help you write healthful menus for breakfast, lunch, and dinner for one week. Share your menus with your family or classmates.

CREATE A MURAL

IN YOUR OWN SCHOOLYARD

Take a walk outside around your school with your teacher and classmates. Take notes on the different plants and animals you see. With classmates, create a mural showing the food chain in your area. Display the mural in class.

CORNER

WHAT DO YOU THINK?

- How do different kinds of animals "balance" each other?

- Would you like to have a backyard like the one you read about? Why or why not?

- What would happen if there were no birds in the backyard? How do you know?

ALL EYES ON

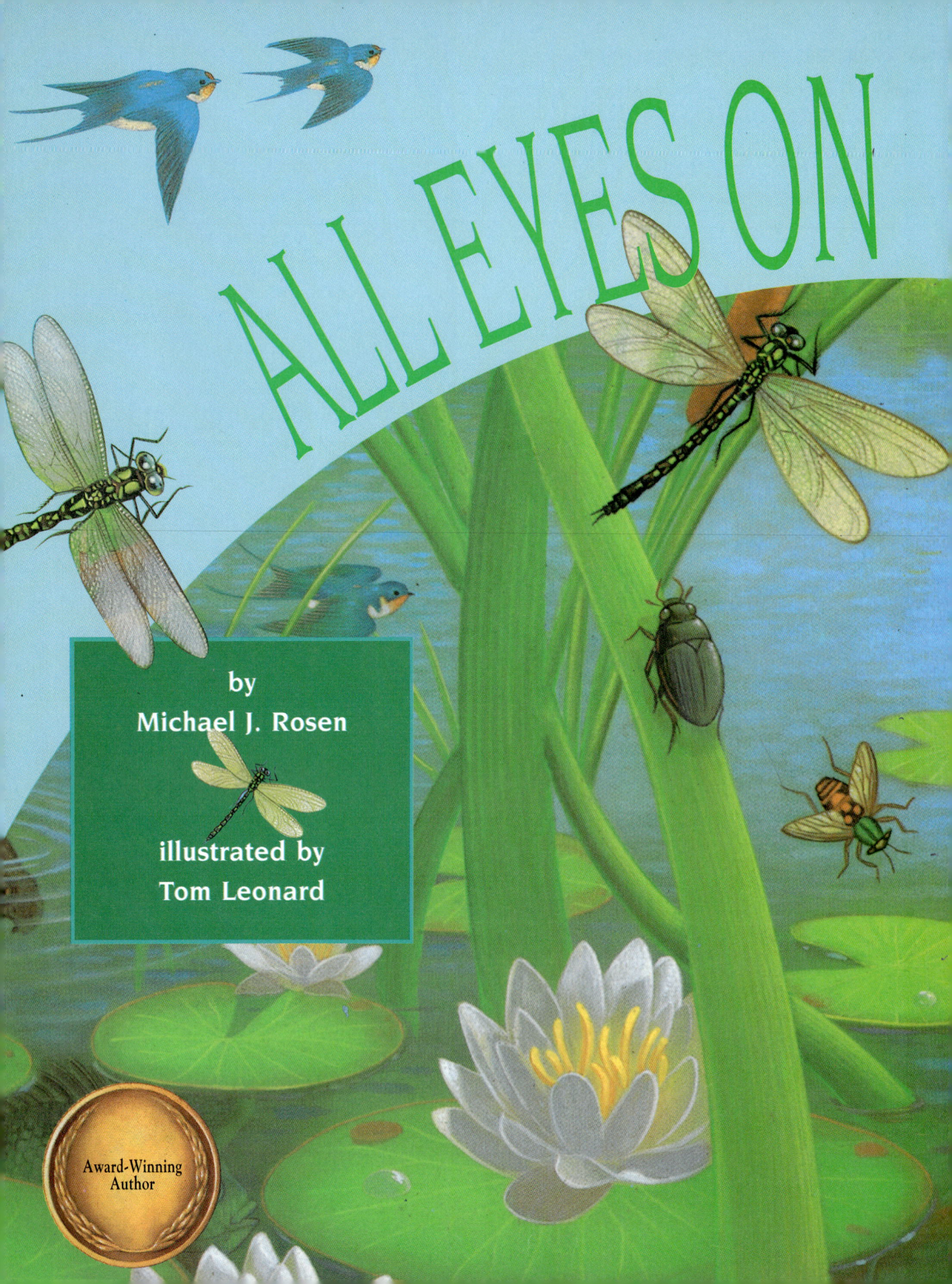

by
Michael J. Rosen

illustrated by
Tom Leonard

Award-Winning Author

THE POND

Here and there around this pond, countless eyes watch what goes on. Listen. They're all calling you: *Come closer, look! Come see my view.*

A world of water multiplies
within the eyes of dragonflies,
whose gazes are kaleidoscopes
that spy atop the cattail slopes.

The snapping turtle sometimes sees
the muddy deep, sometimes the trees,
and sometimes nothing but inside
the painted shell where it can hide.

From where the spider always clings
the view is largely tangled things
dangling in the crisscrossed strands
that weave the windows where it stands.

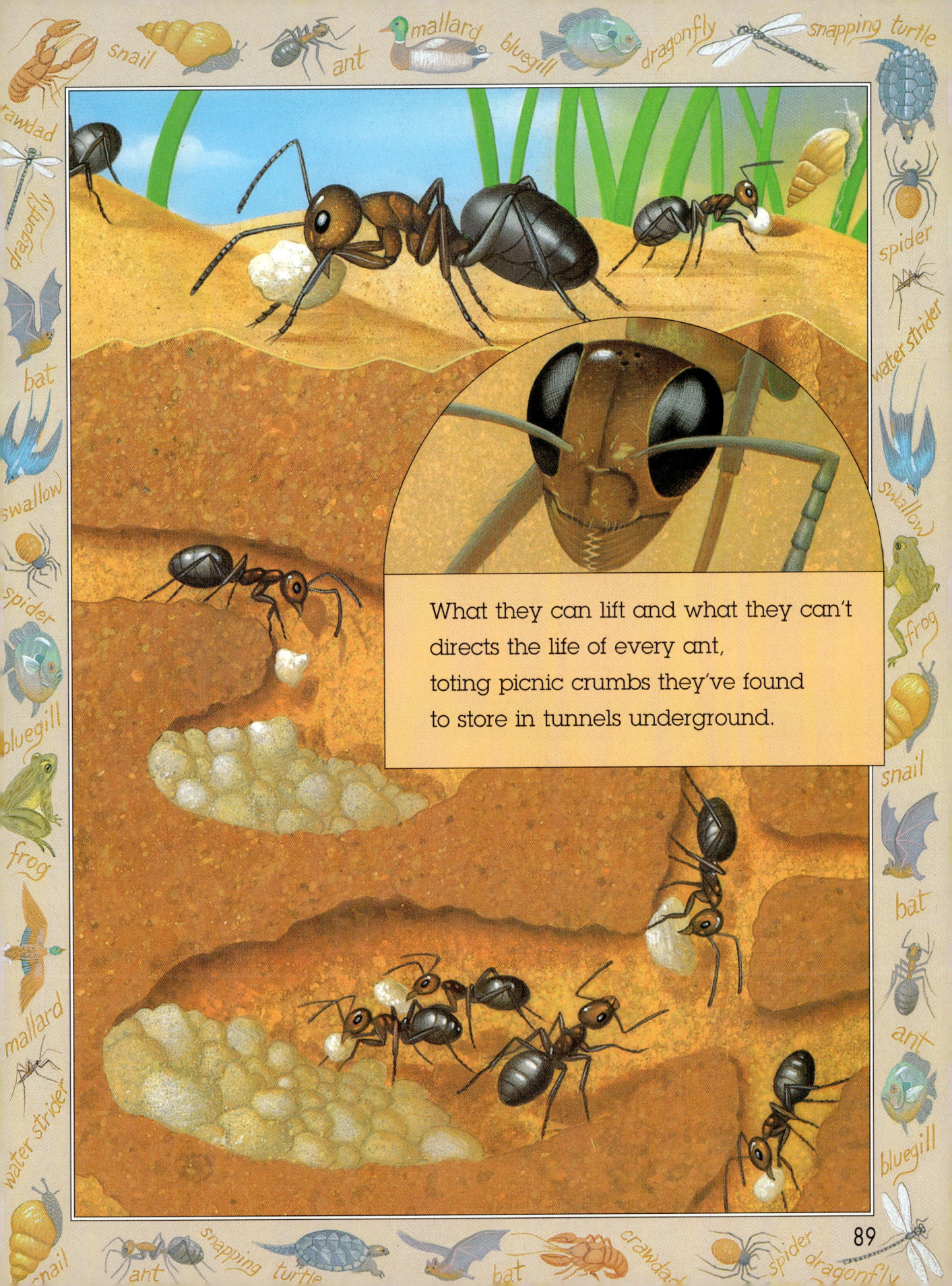

What they can lift and what they can't
directs the life of every ant,
toting picnic crumbs they've found
to store in tunnels underground.

The snail sees simply what it's on
as it glides up a stalk or frond.
Where next? The snail can still decide
as it glides down the other side.

The water strider walks the shine
where air and water form a line.
What's up above? What's down below?
It never has the chance to know.

With echoes bouncing through the night,
the bat can see without its sight.
Soundless shadows, hidden prey—
a bat may swoop and snatch away.

93

To what's ahead, the crawdad's blind.
It only sees what's left behind.
Whooshing backward by its tail,
the crawdad leaves a cloudy trail.

Peering toward the breezy air
where clouds are what the branches bear,
the bluegill watches at the brink
the flitting things it hopes will sink.

There . . . beside the fallen log,
the yellow peepers of a frog
who waits beside an old tree trunk,
nabs a fly, and jumps, *kerplunk*.

97

Paddling through the cattail shoots,
lily pads and toppled roots,
a mallard dips and dives and dunks
to munch upon the duckweed clumps.

Chittering swallows skitter so fast
and skim the waves as they soar past,
keeping an eye on all that's afloat—
a branch, a beetle, an anchored boat.

frog · water strider · swallow · crawdad · spider · mallard · snail

ant · bat · snail · swallow · dragonfly · bluegill · mallard

snapping turtle · water strider · ant · crawdad · snail · bluegill · mallard

The pond itself, seen from the sky,
appears to be a giant's eye.
What's it watching, staring back?
A storm? The clouds? The zodiac?

frog · water strider · swallow · crawdad · spider · mallard · snail

ant · bat · snail · swallow · dragonfly · bluegill · mallard · snapping turtle · water strider · ant · crawdad · snail · bluegill · mallard

If you were here, what would you spy
with your peculiar human eye?
Shhh. Come closer. What's your view?
All the creatures watch for you.

102

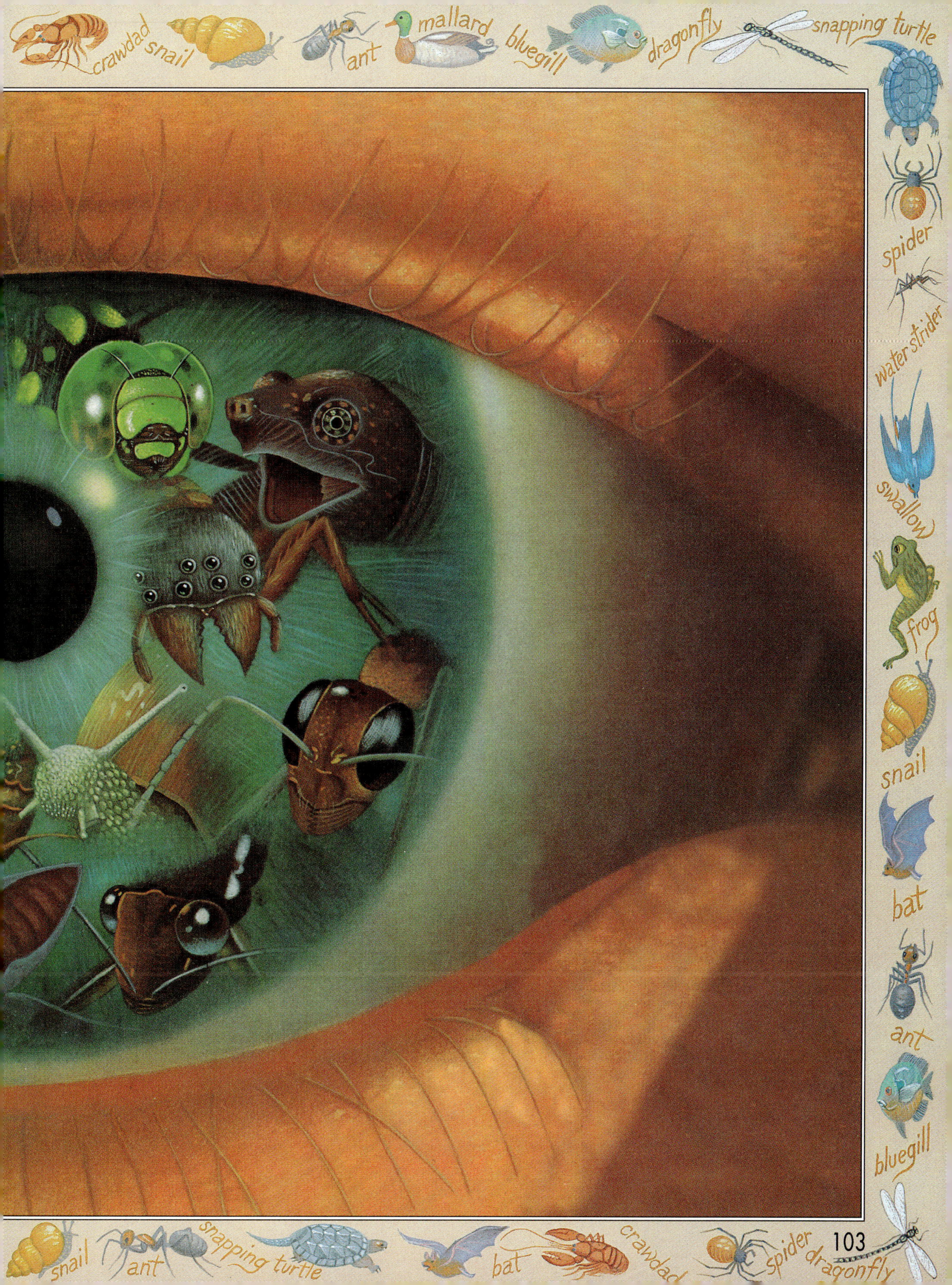
crawdad
snail
ant
mallard
bluegill
dragonfly
snapping turtle
spider
water strider
swallow
frog
snail
bat
ant
bluegill
dragonfly
snail
ant
snapping turtle
bat
crawdad
spider

Meet the Illustrator . . .
Tom Leonard

Ilene Cooper talked to the illustrator of *All Eyes on the Pond.*

Ilene Cooper: *A book like this must take a lot of research.*

Tom Leonard: Yes. I spent about four months in libraries, looking at pictures. I took photographs at ponds and used them when I drew the plants and animals.

Cooper: *How did you decide on the way you would draw the illustrations for this book?*

Leonard: The title is *All Eyes on the Pond,* so I decided that eyes should be an important part of the book. I added a big eye above each word box. Then I added a curve to the box so that it was the shape of a human eye.

Cooper: *How did you get started drawing?*

Leonard: I was a cartoonist when I was young. After graduating from art school, I worked for newspapers and textbooks, and now I'm illustrating children's books. This is only my second one.

Meet the Author...
Michael J. Rosen

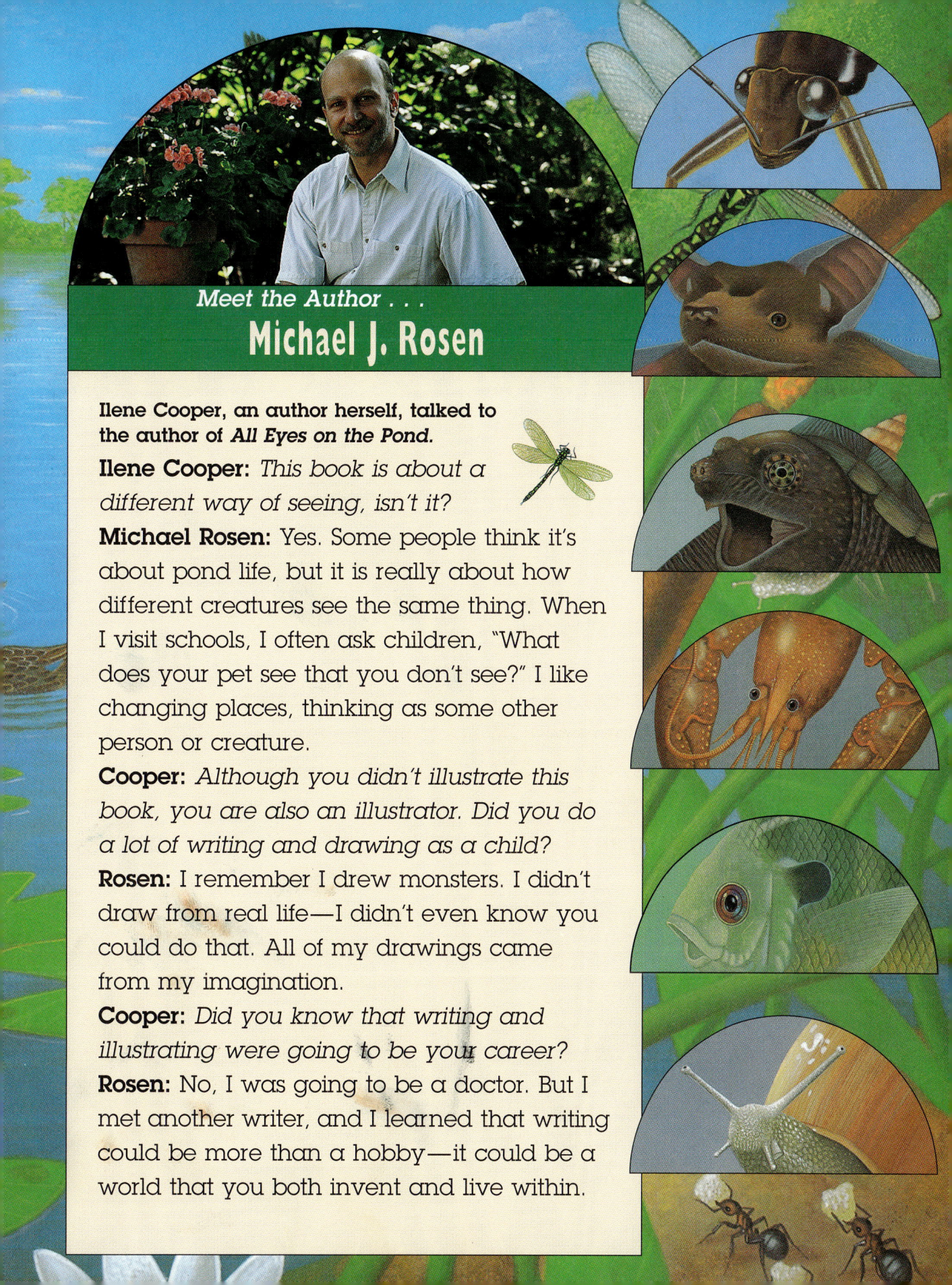

Ilene Cooper, an author herself, talked to the author of *All Eyes on the Pond.*

Ilene Cooper: *This book is about a different way of seeing, isn't it?*

Michael Rosen: Yes. Some people think it's about pond life, but it is really about how different creatures see the same thing. When I visit schools, I often ask children, "What does your pet see that you don't see?" I like changing places, thinking as some other person or creature.

Cooper: *Although you didn't illustrate this book, you are also an illustrator. Did you do a lot of writing and drawing as a child?*

Rosen: I remember I drew monsters. I didn't draw from real life—I didn't even know you could do that. All of my drawings came from my imagination.

Cooper: *Did you know that writing and illustrating were going to be your career?*

Rosen: No, I was going to be a doctor. But I met another writer, and I learned that writing could be more than a hobby—it could be a world that you both invent and live within.

RESPONSE

WRITE A POEM
A Bug's-Eye View

Pond insects see the world in their own ways. How do insects in other environments see things? Pick a common insect that lives in a forest, field, desert, or swamp. Write a poem about how it sees its environment.

DRAW SKETCHES
A Nature Study

Find a quiet spot where you can observe a pet or another animal. Bring a sketch pad and a pencil or charcoal and draw several sketches of the animal. Choose your favorite sketch, and add color with paint or markers to create the finished picture. Then write one or two sentences telling what you learned about the animal.

CORNER

PREPARE A REPORT

All About Eyesight

Animals see differently because their eyes are built differently. How are human eyes built? Work with a partner to prepare a short oral report about human eyes. Use pictures, charts, and other aids to make your report more interesting.

What Do You Think?

- Why do the different animals who live near the pond see different things?
- Which pond animal is your favorite? Why?
- What would you *hear* if you visited a pond? Describe the sounds some of the animals might make.

107

THEME WRAP-UP

All living things—wild and tame, predators and prey—are part of the balance of nature. How is this fact shown in the selection "Wolves"? How is it shown in "Nature's Great Balancing Act"?

Understanding how animals live is important. What did you think of wolves before you read these stories, and what do you think of them now? Have you changed your mind about wolves? Explain your answer.

ACTIVITY CORNER

Choose an animal that must eat other animals to live. Read about the animal in an encyclopedia or a nonfiction book. Then write a short report about the animal's habits. Tell where it lives, what it eats, how it sleeps, and any other facts you find interesting.

Glossary

WHAT IS A GLOSSARY?
A glossary is like a small dictionary at the back of a book. It lists some of the words used in the book, along with their pronunciations, their meanings, and other useful information. If you come across a word you don't know as you are reading, you can look up the word in this glossary.

Using the

Like a dictionary, this glossary lists words in alphabetical order. To find a word, look it up by its first letter or letters.

To save time, use the **guide words** at the top of each page. These show you the first and last words on the page. Look at the guide words to see if your word falls between them alphabetically.

Here is an example of a glossary entry:

- This is the entry word. It's the word you look up.
- Look here to find out how to pronounce the word.
- The letter *n.* means the entry word is a noun.
- This is the definition of the entry word.
- Here you'll find other forms of the word.
- This is a sample sentence using the entry word.
- Synonyms of the entry word come right after *syn.*

com•bi•na•tion [kom´bə•nā´shən] *n.* **com•bi•na•tions** A way things are put together: **Fruit juices come in many different *combinations*, such as cranberry and apple or orange and pineapple.** *syn.* mixture

ETYMOLOGY

Etymology is the study or history of how words are developed. Words often have interesting backgrounds that can help you remember what they mean. Look in the margins of the glossary to find the etymologies of certain words.

Here is an example of an etymology:

value The Latin word *valēre* means "to be strong." The Old French language used this word to make the word *value*, changing the meaning to "worth."

Glossary

PRONUNCIATION

The pronunciation in brackets is a respelling that shows how the word is pronounced.

The **pronunciation key** explains what the symbols in a respelling mean. A shortened pronunciation key appears on every other page of the glossary.

PRONUNCIATION KEY*

a	add, map	m	move, seem	u	up, done
ā	ace, rate	n	nice, tin	û(r)	burn, term
â(r)	care, air	ng	ring, song	yōō	fuse, few
ä	palm, father	o	odd, hot	v	vain, eve
b	bat, rub	ō	open, so	w	win, away
ch	check, catch	ô	order, jaw	y	yet, yearn
d	dog, rod	oi	oil, boy	z	zest, muse
e	end, pet	ou	pout, now	zh	vision, pleasure
ē	equal, tree	ŏŏ	took, full	ə	the schwa, an unstressed vowel representing the sound spelled
f	fit, half	ōō	pool, food		
g	go, log	p	pit, stop		
h	hope, hate	r	run, poor		
i	it, give	s	see, pass		*a* in *above*
ī	ice, write	sh	sure, rush		*e* in *sicken*
j	joy, ledge	t	talk, sit		*i* in *possible*
k	cool, take	th	thin, both		*o* in *melon*
l	look, rule	t̶h̶	this, bathe		*u* in *circus*

Other symbols:
- separates words into syllables
- ´ indicates heavier stress on a syllable
- ` indicates light stress on a syllable

Abbreviations: *adj.* adjective, *adv.* adverb, *conj.* conjunction, *interj.* interjection, *n.* noun, *prep.* preposition, *pron.* pronoun, *syn.* synonym, *v.* verb.

*The Pronunciation Key, adapted entries, and the Short Key that appear on the following pages are reprinted from *HBJ School Dictionary* Copyright © 1990 by Harcourt Brace & Company. Reprinted by permission of Harcourt Brace & Company.

affect

amount
Amount comes from the Latin word meaning "to the mountain" or "upward." An *amount* may be the total number when counting upward or adding.

A

af·fect
[ə·fekt′] *v.* **af·fects** To change; to cause something else to happen: **This experiment shows how sunlight *affects* the growth of plants.** *syn.* influence

al·low·ance
[ə·lou′əns] *n.* A set sum of money a person gets regularly, such as each week: **Gordon gets an *allowance* of five dollars every week.**

a·mount
[ə·mount′] *n.* A certain number of something; a sum: **The *amount* of money I had was not enough to buy the poster.** *syn.* quantity

anx·ious
[angk′shəs] *adj.* Worried; uneasy: **Valerie was *anxious* about oversleeping because she thought she might miss the school bus.**

ar·rive
[ə·rīv′] *v.* **ar·rived** To get to a place: **Ivan *arrived* at the game at four o'clock.** *syn.* reach

as·ton·ish
[ə·ston′ish] *v.* **as·ton·ished** To surprise; to fill with wonder: **It was a clear night, and the number of stars in the sky *astonished* him.** *syn.* amaze

B

blind
[blīnd] *adj.* Unable to see: **Most fish that live in dark caves are *blind*.**

brace

[brās] *v.* **braced** To prepare for something that might be bad; to hold oneself tightly in place: **Ryan held onto a pole on the bus as he *braced* himself for a sudden stop.**

buck·et

[buk´it] *n.* **buck·ets** A round container with a flat bottom and a curved handle, used to carry things: **Shelly filled two *buckets* with water, got some soap and a mop, and was ready to wash the floor.** *syn.* pail

C

cab·in

[kab´in] *n.* A small wooden house, sometimes made of big logs: **Our family stays in a *cabin* by a lake every summer.** *syn.* hut

car·pen·ter

[kär´pən·tər] *n.* A person who makes things out of wood: **The *carpenter* made a bookcase for our room.**

child·hood

[chīld´hood´] *n.* The time when someone is young: **Tara had a very happy *childhood* and always played with her friends.** *syn.* youth

choice

[chois] *n.* **choic·es** The act of picking which one: **There were many *choices* to make at the bakery, but we decided to get muffins and apple tarts.** *syns.* decision, selection

choice

bucket The Old English word *buc* also means "belly." A *bucket* is a container that holds things, just as a belly is a container that holds food.

cabin

a	add	oo	took
ā	ace	o͞o	pool
â	care	u	up
ä	palm	û	burn
e	end	yo͞o	fuse
ē	equal	oi	oil
i	it	ou	pout
ī	ice	ng	ring
o	odd	th	thin
ō	open	th	this
ô	order	zh	vision

ə = { *a* in *above*, *e* in *sicken*, *i* in *possible*, *o* in *melon*, *u* in *circus* }

337

combination

comfortable
This word comes from *comfort*, which used to mean "strong." In the 1800s, its meaning changed and became "at ease."

creek

com·bi·na·tion
[kom´bə·nā´shən] *n.* **com·bi·na·tions** A way things are put together: **Fruit juices come in many different *combinations*, such as cranberry and apple or orange and pineapple.** *syn.* mixture

com·fort·a·ble
[kum´fər·tə·bəl] *adj.* Restful; at ease: **In the summer, José feels *comfortable* in his air-conditioned house.**

com·mer·cial
[kə·mûr´shəl] *n.* An advertisement on television or radio, used for selling something: **The *commercial* for the new cereal made Kelly feel hungry.**

con·grat·u·la·tions
[kən·grach´ə·lā´shənz] *n.* Good wishes letting someone know you are happy for him or her: **Congratulations on your team's great game!**

crea·ture
[krē´chər] *n.* **crea·tures** An animal: **Many different *creatures* live in the rain forest.**

creek
[krēk or krik] *n.* A small, narrow river that may not be very deep: **The cowboy got fresh water for his horse from the *creek*.** *syn.* stream

cu·ri·ous
[kyoor´ē·əs] *adj.* Wanting to know or find out more: **Elena was *curious* and wanted to learn how rainbows are formed.** *syn.* questioning

D

depth
[depth] *n.* **depths** A far distance into something; the part deep down: **The sunken ship was lost in the *depths* of the sea.**

des•ti•na•tion
[des´tə•nā´shən] *n.* The place someone is going to; a goal: **The *destination* of our trip was New York City, and we were eager to get there.**

de•stroy
[di•stroi´] *v.* **de•stroyed** To put an end to; to break something apart so badly that it cannot be fixed: **After the storm, our garden was *destroyed* and we had to replant everything.** *syns.* ruin, wreck

dor•mant
[dôr´mənt] *adj.* Not moving or growing for a period of time; at rest: **The plants under the snow are *dormant*, but they will grow again in the spring.** *syn.* asleep

E

earn
[ûrn] *v.* **earned** To get as payment for hard work: **Han *earned* some money by washing cars.** *syn.* gain

ech•o
[ek´ō] *n.* **ech•oes** A sound that comes back again: **Tommy shouted into the cave and heard the *echoes* of his voice come back softer and softer, again and again.** *syn.* repetition

echo

depths *Depth* comes from the word *deep*. *Deep* comes from a word that means "diving duck." Many words have come from *deep*, such as *dimple*, *dip*, and *dive*.

earn

a	add	o͝o	took
ā	ace	o͞o	pool
â	care	u	up
ä	palm	û	burn
e	end	yo͞o	fuse
ē	equal	oi	oil
i	it	ou	pout
ī	ice	ng	ring
o	odd	th	thin
ō	open	t̶h̶	this
ô	order	zh	vision

ə = { *a* in *above*, *e* in *sicken*, *i* in *possible*, *o* in *melon*, *u* in *circus* }

339

emperor

graze

hesitate
Hesitate once meant "to become stuck." It now means "to pause or wait."

em•per•or
[em′pər•ər] *n.* A person who rules a land: **The *emperor* lived in a beautiful palace, and he made all the laws himself.** *syn.* king

en•er•gy
[en′ər•jē] *n.* The force or power to make things work; the ability to make things go: **Eating breakfast in the morning gives me *energy* to work during the day.**

ex•ist
[ig•zist′] *v.* To be; to live: **Dinosaurs do not *exist* anymore, but we can learn about them in books.**

ex•tinc•tion
[ik•stingk′shən] *n.* When there is no more of a kind of animal or plant: **The white tigers in India are faced with *extinction* because people have hunted them too much.**

G

graze
[grāz] *v.* **graz•ing** To feed on grass: **The cows were *grazing* on the hillside where the grass was thick.**

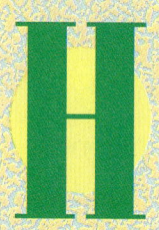

H

hes•i•tate
[hez′ə•tāt′] *v.* To stop and think whether to do or say something: **Carol saw her father *hesitate* before he bought the purple lamp.** *syns.* pause, delay

home•sick
[hōm′sik′] *adj.* Sad because you miss your family and the place you live: **Aretha was very *homesick* while she was at overnight camp.** *syn.* lonely

340

I

i·den·ti·fy
[ī·den´tə·fī] *v.*
i·den·ti·fied To see and know by name; to point out: **Julian *identified* three butterflies while on a field trip to the park.** *syn.* recognize

im·age
[im´ij] *n.* A picture or likeness of, as seen in a mirror: **Katy saw her *image* reflected in the store window.** *syn.* appearance

im·pa·tience
[im·pā´shəns] *n.* A feeling of not wanting to wait; not wanting things to slow down: **Sam made a mistake on the test because of his *impatience* to be the first one done.** *syn.* eagerness

L

ledge
[lej] *n.* A narrow, flat shelf that sticks out from a steep rock or wall: **Carlos put some flowerpots on the *ledge* outside the window.**

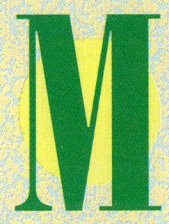

M

man·ners
[man´ərz] *n.* Polite ways to do things; ways to do things that show good behavior: **My mother taught me the good *manners* to always say "Please" and "Thank you."** *syn.* etiquette

mol·ten
[mōl´tən] *adj.* Made into a hot liquid by heat: **When a volcano becomes active, *molten* rock, or lava, flows out of it.**

molten

ledge

molten *Molten* is from the word *melt*. The first meaning of *melt* was "soft." When something *melts*, it usually becomes a liquid or a "soft" substance.

a	add	o͝o	took
ā	ace	o͞o	pool
â	care	u	up
ä	palm	û	burn
e	end	yo͞o	fuse
ē	equal	oi	oil
i	it	ou	pout
ī	ice	ng	ring
o	odd	th	thin
ō	open	ᵺ	this
ô	order	zh	vision

ə = {
a in *above*
e in *sicken*
i in *possible*
o in *melon*
u in *circus*
}

341

N

ner·vous
[nûr´vəs] *adj.* Worried and somewhat fearful: **I felt *nervous* about singing in front of the class, but I did it anyway.** *syn.* uneasy

O

or·bit
[ôr´bit] *v.* **orbits** To move around another object, usually in space: **The Earth *orbits* the sun once a year.** *syn.* circle

P

pave
[pāv] *v.* **paved** To cover an area of ground with something hard, such as concrete: **The street in front of my house was once dirt, but it was *paved* last week.**

pe·cul·iar
[pi·kyōōl´yər] *adj.* Belonging to only one person or thing; strange or unusual: **Jennifer had a *peculiar* dog that ate carrots.** *syns.* unique, odd

peer
[pir] *v.* **peer·ing** To look closer to see more clearly: **Billy was *peering* under the bed, looking for his shoes.**

---

peculiar
Peculiar comes from a Latin word meaning "private property." *Pecu* meant "cattle," and years ago cattle were very important property. The meaning then changed to "belonging only to oneself." In English, it came to mean "being the only one of its kind."

pop•u•la•tion
[pop′yə•lā′shən] *n.*
pop•u•la•tions A group or kind; a certain group of people or animals living in one place: **Some owl *populations* are in danger because people are cutting down too many of the trees that they live in.** *syn.* inhabitants

post•card
[pōst′kärd′] *n.*
post•cards A stiff, rectangular piece of paper with a picture on one side and writing space on the other side, made to be sent through the mail: **While Carmen was traveling with her parents, she kept in touch with her friends by sending them *postcards*.**

R

re•ceive
[ri•sēv′] *v.* To get something, as in a gift: **I will *receive* 5 cents for every soda can I turn in.** *syns.* acquire, obtain

re•mind
[ri•mīnd′] *v.* **re•mind•ed** To cause to remember; to make someone think of something again: **The tacos *reminded* Jane of her trip to Mexico and of the wonderful food she ate there.**

S

sax•o•phone
[sak′sə•fōn′] *n.* A musical instrument in the shape of a curved brass tube: **Mike plays a *saxophone* in the band.**

saxophone

saxophone

a	add	o͝o	took
ā	ace	o͞o	pool
â	care	u	up
ä	palm	û	burn
e	end	yo͞o	fuse
ē	equal	oi	oil
i	it	ou	pout
ī	ice	ng	ring
o	odd	th	thin
ō	open	t͟h	this
ô	order	zh	vision

ə = { *a* in *above*
e in *sicken*
i in *possible*
o in *melon*
u in *circus* }

343

seacoast

soldier The Latin word *solidus* means "military pay." French changed it to *solde*, and the person getting the military pay was called a *soldior*. English changed it to *soldier*.

soldier

sea·coast
[sē´kōst´] *n.* The area where the land meets the ocean: **When walking along the *seacoast*, it is fun to watch the waves.** *syns.* shore, beach

silk
[silk] *n.* A kind of cloth made from a strong, shiny, threadlike material: **Suki likes scarves made of *silk* because they feel so smooth.**

sol·dier
[sōl´jər] *n.* **sol·diers** A person in the army; someone who watches over others and keeps them from harm: **The *soldiers* guard the queen when she is outside the palace.** *syns.* protector, fighter

spy
[spī] *v.* To watch closely without being seen: **The little kids always *spy* on us because they want to find our secret clubhouse.**

sur·face
[sûr´fis] *n.* The outer part of something; the outer layer that covers something: **The *surface* of the moon is rocky and dry.**

sur·vive
[sər·vīv´] *v.* To live through; to stay alive: **Dolphins need to come up for air in order to *survive* in the ocean.** *syn.* remain

swal·low
[swol´ō] *v.* To make something go down the throat and into the stomach: **I try to chew my food well, so it will be easy to *swallow*.**

T

tame
[tām] *adj.* Under control, not wild: **The *tame* animals in the petting zoo will not bite.**
syn. gentle

throne
[thrōn] *n.* A chair for a ruler: **The king sat on his *throne* as the crown was placed on his head.**

U

un·der·ground
[un´dər·ground´] *adj.* Below the earth: **We went into the tunnel and rode the *underground* train.**

uni·verse
[yōō´nə·vûrs´] *n.* Everything in the world; the sun, stars, and planets: **Astronauts see parts of the *universe* that cannot be seen from Earth.**

V

val·ue
[val´yōō] *n.* The worth; the price: **This painting has great *value* because the painter is famous.**
syn. cost

view
[vyōō] *n.* What can be seen from a place: **I have a *view* of the street from my window.**

Y

yawn
[yôn] *v.* To open the mouth wide when one is sleepy: **Tyrone was sleepy and he soon began to *yawn*.**

yawn

throne

value The Latin word *valēre* means "to be strong." The Old French language used this word to make the word *value*, changing the meaning to "worth."

a	add	o͝o	took
ā	ace	o͞o	pool
â	care	u	up
ä	palm	û	burn
e	end	yōō	fuse
ē	equal	oi	oil
i	it	ou	pout
ī	ice	ng	ring
o	odd	th	thin
ō	open	t̶h̶	this
ô	order	zh	vision

ə = { *a* in *above*
e in *sicken*
i in *possible*
o in *melon*
u in *circus* }

345

INDEX OF Titles and Authors

Page numbers in color refer to biographical information.

Aardema, Verna, **18,** *34*

All Eyes on the Pond, **84**

Amber Brown Is Not a Crayon, **190**

Borreguita and the Coyote, **18**

Bug Sat in a Silver Flower, A, **80**

Carrison, Muriel Paskin, **314**

Class Act, A, **272**

Cleary, Beverly, **316,** *329*

Creative Minds at Work, **266**

Danziger, Paula, **190,** *199*

Garland, Sherry, **166,** *185*

Gibbons, Gail, **38,** *49*

Godkin, Celia, **54**

Grandfather's Journey, **130**

Houston, Gloria, **114,** *127*

Hubbell, Patricia, **258**

I Am Flying!, **256**

If You Made a Million, **278**

Inventor Thinks Up Helicopters, The, **258**

Journey Through the Solar System, **226**

King and the Poor Boy, The, **314**

Kuskin, Karla, **80**

Lotus Seed, The, **166**

Marzollo, Jean, **266**

Millay, Edna St. Vincent, **163**

My Great-Aunt Arizona, **114**

Nature's Great Balancing Act, **64**

Norsgaard, E. Jaediker, **64**

Patently Ridiculous, **262**

Prelutsky, Jack, **256**

Prince, Saul T., **262**

Ramona and Her Father, **316**

Rochelle, Belinda, **202**, **217**

Rosen, Michael J., **84**, **105**

Say, Allen, **130**, **160**

Schwartz, David M., **278**, **310**

Stannard, Russell, **226**

That Mountain Far Away, **162**

Travel, **163**

When Jo Louis Won the Title, **202**

Wolf Island, **54**

Wolves, **38**

Copyright © 1997 by Harcourt Brace & Company

All rights reserved. No part of this publication may be reproduced or transmitted in any form or by any means, electronic or mechanical, including photocopy, recording, or any information storage and retrieval system, without permission in writing from the publisher.

Requests for permission to make copies of any part of the work should be mailed to: Permissions Department, Harcourt Brace & Company, 6277 Sea Harbor Drive, Orlando, Florida 32887-6777.

HARCOURT BRACE and Quill Design is a registered trademark of Harcourt Brace & Company.

Printed in the United States of America

Acknowledgments

For permission to reprint copyrighted material, grateful acknowledgment is made to the following sources:

Beautiful America Publishing Company: Cover illustration by Carol Johnson from *A Journey of Hope/Una Jornada de Esperanza* by Bob Harvey and Diane Kelsay Harvey. Copyright 1991 by Little America Publishing Co.

Curtis Brown Ltd.: Corrected galley from *Borreguita and the Coyote* by Verna Aardema. Originally published in *A Bookworm Who Hatched*, Richard C. Owen Publishers, Inc., 1993.

Children's Television Workshop: "Patently Ridiculous" by Saul T. Prince, illustrated by John Lawrence/Bernstein & Associates from *3-2-1 Contact Magazine*, May 1994. Copyright 1994 by Children's Television Workshop. "A Class Act" from *Kid City Magazine*, March 1993. Text copyright 1993 by Children's Television Workshop.

Dial Books for Young Readers, a division of Penguin Books USA Inc.: Cover illustration by Jerry Pinkney from *Back Home* by Gloria Jean Pinkney. Illustration copyright © 1992 by Jerry Pinkney.

Dutton Signet, a division of Penguin Books USA Inc.: From *Nature's Great Balancing Act in Our Own Backyard* by E. Jaediker Norsgaard, photographs by Campbell Norsgaard. Text copyright © 1990 by E. Jaediker Norsgaard; photographs copyright © 1990 by Campbell Norsgaard.

*Fitzhenry & Whiteside, Limited, Markham, Ontario:*ced by *Wolf Island* by Celia Godkin. Copyright © 1989 by Celia Godkin.

Greenwillow Books, a division of William Morrow & Company, Inc.: Cover illustration by Jim Fowler from *Dolphin Adventure: A True Story* by Wayne Grover. Illustration copyright © 1990 by Jim Fowler. "I Am Flying" from *The New Kid on the Block* by Jack Prelutsky, cover illustration by James Stevenson. Text copyright © 1984 by Jack Prelutsky; cover illustration copyright © 1984 by James Stevenson.

Grosset & Dunlap, Inc., a division of The Putnam & Grosset Group: Cover illustration by Paige Billin-Frye from *What's Out There? A Book About Space* by Lynn Wilson. Illustration copyright © 1993 by Paige Billin-Frye.

Harcourt Brace & Company: Cover illustration by Greg Shed from *Dandelions* by Eve Bunting. Illustration copyright © 1995 by Greg Shed. *The Lotus Seed* by Sherry Garland, illustrated by Tatsuro Kiuchi. Text copyright © 1993 by Sherry Garland; illustrations copyright © 1993 by Tatsuro Kiuchi.

HarperCollins Publishers: *My Great-Aunt Arizona* by Gloria Houston, illustrated by Susan Condie Lamb. Text copyright © 1992 by Gloria Houston; illustrations copyright © 1992 by Susan Condie Lamb. "A Bug Sat in a Silver Flower" from *Dogs & Dragons, Trees & Dreams* by Karla Kuskin. Text copyright © 1980 by Karla Kuskin. Cover illustration by Kam Mak from *The Year of the Panda* by Miriam Schlein. Illustraton copyright © 1990 by Kam Mak.

Holiday House, Inc.: *Wolves* by Gail Gibbons. Copyright © 1994 by Gail Gibbons.

Henry Holt and Company: Cover illustration by Cat Bowman Smith from *Max Malone Makes a Million* by Charlotte Herman. Illustration copyright © 1991 by Catherine Bowman Smith.

Houghton Mifflin Company: Cover illustration by Karen M. Dugan from *Halmoni and the Picnic* by Sook Nyul Choi. Illustration copyright © 1993 by Karen Milone Dugan. *When Jo Louis Won the Title* by Belinda Rochelle, illustrated by Larry Johnson. Text copyright © 1994 by Belinda Rochelle; illustrations copyright © 1994 by Larry Johnson. *Grandfather's Journey* by Allen Say. Copyright © 1993 by Allen Say.

Hyperion Books For Children: *All Eyes on the Pond* by Michael J. Rosen, illustrated by Tom Leonard. Text copyright © 1994 by Michael J. Rosen; illustrations © 1994 by Tom Leonard.

Alfred A. Knopf, Inc.: *Borreguita and the Coyote* by Verna Aardema, illustrated by Petra Mathers. Text copyright © 1991 by Verna Aardema; illustrations copyright © 1991 by Petra Mathers.

Larousse Kingfisher Chambers Inc., New York: From *Our Universe: A Guide To What's Out There* (Retitled: "Journey Through the Solar System") by Russell Stannard, illustrated by Michael Bennallack-Hart, Helen Floate, and Diana Mayo. Text copyright © 1995 by Russell Stannard; illustrations copyright © 1995 by Larousse plc.

Lee & Low Books, Inc.: Cover illustration by Cornelius Van Wright and Ying-Hwa Hu from *Sam and the Lucky Money* by Karen Chinn. Illustration copyright © 1995 by Cornelius Van Wright and Ying-Hwa Hu.

Lerner Publications Company, Minneapolis, MN: Cover photograph by Jake Rajs from *The Statue of Liberty: America's Proud Lady* by Jim Haskins. Copyright © 1986 by Jim Haskins.

Lothrop, Lee & Shepard Books, a division of William Morrow & Company, Inc.: *If You Made a Million* by David M. Schwartz, illustrated by Steven Kellogg. Text copyright © 1989 by David M. Schwartz; illustrations copyright © 1989 by Steven Kellogg; photographs of money copyright © 1989 by George Ancona.

Morrow Junior Books, a division of William Morrow & Company, Inc.: From *Ramona and Her Father* by Beverly Cleary. Text copyright © 1975, 1977 by Beverly Cleary. Cover illustration by Louis Darling from *Ellen Tebbits* by Beverly Cleary. Copyright 1951 by Beverly Cleary. Cover illustration by Alan Tiegreen from *Ramona the Brave* by Beverly Cleary. Copyright © 1975 by Beverly Cleary. Cover illustration by Louis Darling from *The Mouse and the Motorcycle* by Beverly Cleary. Copyright © 1965 by Beverly Cleary. Cover illustration by Beatrice Darwin from *Socks* by Beverly Cleary. Copyright © 1973 by Beverly Cleary. Cover illustration by Louis Darling from *Henry and the Clubhouse* by Beverly Cleary. Copyright © 1962 by Beverly Cleary. Cover illustration by Louis Darling from *Otis Spofford* by Beverly Cleary. Copyright 1953 by Beverly Cleary. Cover illustration by Kay Life from *Muggie Maggie* by Beverly Cleary. Illustration copyright © 1990 by William Morrow and Company, Inc.

G. P. Putnam's Sons: From *Amber Brown Is Not a Crayon* by Paula Danziger, illustrated by Tony Ross. Text copyright © 1994 by Paula Danziger; illustrations copyright © 1994 by Tony Ross. Cover illustration by Tony Ross from *Amber Brown Goes Fourth* by Paula Danziger. Illustration copyright © 1995 by Tony Ross.

Random House, Inc.: Cover illustration by Dora Leder from *Julian's Glorious Summer* by Ann Cameron. Illustration copyright © 1987 by Dora Leder. Cover illustration by Arnold Lobel from *The Random House Book of Poetry for Children*, selected by Jack Prelutsky. Copyright © 1983 by Random House, Inc.

Marian Reiner, on behalf of Patricia Hubbell and Ju-Hong Chen: "The Inventor Thinks Up Helicopters" from *The Tigers Brought Pink Lemonade* by Patricia Hubbell, illustrated by Ju-Hong Chen. Text copyright © 1988 by Patricia Hubbell; illustrations copyright © 1988 by Ju-Hong Chen.

Scholastic Inc.: Cover illustration from *All About Alligators* by Jim Arnosky. Copyright © 1994 by Jim Arnosky. From *My First Book of Biographies* (Retitled: "Creative Minds at Work") by Jean Marzollo. Text copyright © 1994 by Jean Marzollo.

Charles E. Tuttle Company, Inc.: "The King and the Poor Boy" from *Cambodian Folk Stories from the Gatiloke*, retold by Muriel Paskin Carrison, from a translation by The Venerable Kong Chhean. Text © 1987 by Charles E. Tuttle Publishing Co., Inc.

Viking Penguin, a division of Penguin Books USA Inc.: Cover illustration by Susanna Natti from *Cam Jansen and the Mystery of the Television Dog* by David A. Adler. Illustration copyright © 1981 by Susanna Natti.

Dinh D. Vu: "Nothing that grows..."/"Hoa Sen" from *The Lotus Seed* by Sherry Garland.

Walker Books Limited, London: Cover illustration from *When Hunger Calls* by Bert Kitchen. Copyright © 1994 by Bert Kitchen. Originally published in the United States by Candlewick Press, Cambridge, MA.

Every effort has been made to locate the copyright holders for the selections in this work. The publishers would be pleased to receive information that would allow the corrections of any omissions in future printings.

Photo Credits

Key: (t) top, (b) bottom, (c) center, (l) left, (r) right, (bg) background, (i) inset

John Lei/OPC, 18, 55, 199(bg), 200-201; Melody Norsgaard/Newcombe Productions, 64-65; Herb Segars/Animals Animals. 68; Stephen Dalton/Photo Researchers, 70; Art Wolfe/Tony Stone Images, 71; Dwight Kuhn/Bruce Coleman, Inc., 72; Laura Riley/Bruce Coleman, Inc. 73(t), 77(b); E. R. Degginger/Animals Animals, 73(b); W. Bayer/Bruce Coleman, Inc., 74-75; S. Nielsen/Bruce Coleman, Inc, 76; Joe McDonald/Animals Animals, 77(t); Phil Degginger/Bruce Coleman, Inc., 78; Keith Gunnar/Bruce Coleman, Inc, 78-79; Robert P. Carr/Bruce Coleman, Inc., 79; Sal DiMarco/Black Star/Harcourt Brace & Company, 104; Wes Bobbitt/Black Star/Harcourt Brace & Company, 127; Culver Pictures, 130-131(bg), 160-161(bg), 164-165(bg); Dale Higgins/Harcourt Brace & Company, 160; Bob Newey, 199; Dennis Brack/Black Star/Harcourt Brace & Company, 217(t); Rick Friedman/Black Star/Harcourt Brace & Company, 217(b) Richard B. Levine, 218(t), Debra P. Hershkowitz, 218(b); Jeff Greenberg/Photo Researchers, 219(t), 219(b); Superstock, 226-227, 229(i), 230, 236-237, 239(i), 246-247(b), 260(bg); Earl Young/FPG International, 228-229; Telegraph Colour Library/FPG International, 233, 234-235, 260(b); NASA, 235(i), 238-239, 243-245, 246, 247(b), 248-253, 261(t), 261(c). 261(b); David Hardy/Photo researchers, 254; the Bettmann Archive, 269, 271; Les Morsillo, 274-279

Illustration Credits

Gennady Spirin, Cover Art; Lori Lohstoeder, 6-7, 13-17, 108; Margaret Kasahara, 8-9, 109-110, 113, 220; Wayne Vincent, 10-11, 221-225, 332; Tyrone Geter, title page; Lehner & White, misc. icons; Petra Mathers, 18-37; Gail Gibbons, 38-51; Celia Godkin, 54-63; Tom Leonard, 64-69, 86-87, 92-93, 258-259; Kristin Goeters, 69; Daniel Moreton, 80-81; Tom Leonard, 94-107; Susan Condie Lamb, 114-129; Allen Say, 130-161, 164-165; Arvis Stewart, 161; Tatsuro Kiuchi, 166-187; Paula Danziger, 190-198, 200-201; Larry Johnson, 202-217; Tyrone Geter, 217; Tom Leonard, 256-257; Ju-Hong Chen, 258-295; Hugh Whyte, 268-271; Steven Kellogg, 278-313; R.J. Shay, 316-331

a.

fig. 1 diving beetle
b.

a.

fig. 2 moth
b.

fig. 3 catfish

fig. 4 salamander

fig. 9 mosquito

fig. 10 crawdad

fig. 11 water snake

fig. 12 heron

fig. 18 fly

b.

a.

fig. 20 dragonfly
b.

fig. 19 bat
a.